Advance Praise for
Women in the Higher Education C-Suite: Diverse Executive Profiles

Compelling and insightful, Takami's book showcases the transformative power of authentic women's leadership in higher education, especially in times of crisis. In the process, it serves to inspire the next generation of diverse women leaders, whose voices are more critical than ever.

> *Dr. Lynn Pasquerella*
> *President, American Association*
> *of Colleges & Universities*

Dr. Takami, in sharing her leadership lessons and elevating those of executives she profiles, inspires and encourages the next generation of women leaders in higher education C-suites to prepare and persist. It took significant courage and resilience for the women leaders in this book to share their experience and engagement on difficult topics that resonate with other female leaders. Their experiences pave a wider path for other women leaders to further develop and ultimately succeed.

> *Marion Ross Fedrick, Ed.D.*
> *President, Albany State University*

Lisa Mednick Takami's *Women in the Higher Education C-Suite* aims to help grow diverse leaders by making visible the stories of women including those from African American, Asian American, Latinx, and Native American contexts who occupy the highest roles in higher education. Using their own words, the book shows how claiming one's power can change what leaders look like and how leaders lead in ways we need. Solving challenges by prioritizing one's sensibilities, backgrounds, and approaches opens access to leadership for anyone and everyone who has talent and inclination. Our students deserve leadership that rises to the occasion of diversity to serve and honor the abundance of experiences that our students bring to our institutions today.

> *Celine Parreñas Shimizu, M.F.A., Ph.D.*
> *Dean, Division of the Arts*
> *Distinguished Professor, Department of Film & Digital Media*
> *University of California, Santa Cruz*

Leading from the top of a post-secondary institution is more complicated and nuanced than ever. From these professional heights, there are many traps and tripwires, but they are not experienced universally; in fact, women and people of color have their own unique sets of hurdles to surmount. Dr. Takami's book, *Women in the Higher Education C-Suite: Diverse Executive Profiles* serves as both a window and a mirror for aspiring college and university leaders. Through telling the stories – both the springboards and the hurdles – of eleven skillful, creative, and resourceful women, the reader gains valuable insight into their planned path for success. Dr. Takami's book is an excellent resource, one that will help secure and retain more diverse senior leadership at our colleges and universities.

Dr. Aram deKoven
Chief Diversity Officer

In *Women in the Higher Education C-Suite*, Dr. Takami shares candid profiles of contemporary leaders of higher education who serve as university, college, and professional association presidents, and those who are among the first to serve in *Chief Diversity Officer* positions at their institutions. The artfully crafted profiles share the opportunities and challenges from being the firsts in their roles. Attending to the complexity of intersectionality, Takami brings to light the challenges of being a leader who manages the politics of race and gender. The volume is reminiscent of Astin & Leland's *Women of Influence, Women of Vision*, bringing greater understanding of how this generation's trailblazers have impacted higher education and how their leadership is transforming it.

Dr. Anna Ortiz
Dean, College of Education,
California State University, Long Beach

The brilliance in these voices and in the actions taken by these women demonstrate the diversity in leadership and thought. Dr. Takami provides the reader with an inspirational lens into their personal journeys of strength, resilience, and care for self, others, and the organization. Which is why it is beyond time for a woman to become President and reunite these States.

Mohammed I. T. Bey
Vice President for Institutional Inclusion,
Carroll University

This book is a must-read for anyone looking to take their career to the next level while also making a positive impact on the world around them. One of the book's key messages is the importance of being open to new opportunities and experiences, even if they don't fit neatly into your existing career path. By embracing uncertainty and being willing to take risks, you can discover new passions and talents that can help you grow both personally and professionally. Another powerful message in the book is the importance of using your career to give back to others. Whether through mentorship, volunteering, or other forms of community service, we all have the power to make a positive difference in the world. Finally, this book offers valuable insights for working women who are trying to balance career success with other important priorities, such as family and personal fulfilment. By setting clear priorities and being intentional about how you spend your time, you can achieve a sense of balance and satisfaction that allows you to truly have it all.

Beth Whited
EVP – Sustainability & Strategy,
Chief Human Resource Officer, Union Pacific Railroad

For most of history, those who have held society's reins have understood the power and value of education. For many this education was not available, particularly for the poor and women.

The history of women and higher education reveals that higher education can not only be an instrument of personal opportunity, but also one of societal innovation. Dr. Mildred García's insight – "The only inheritance a poor family can leave you is a good education," and Dr. Joanne Li's leadership motto, "You need to look up, to reflect, and to build connections" – are fundamental truths. As women, we often continue to face obstacles, particularly as we move into leadership roles. The wisdom in this book will be impactful to all executive women and women aspiring to executive leadership positions.

Constance Ryan
CEO, Streck

Lisa Mednick Takami's *Women in the Higher Education C-Suite: Diverse Executive Profiles* masterfully pulls back the veil to showcase the breadth of experiences of women leaders working to improve higher education. These stories in the aggregate model that change will not happen if we spectate. We have to be active participants who strategically bolster partnerships, personify fortitude, and center empathy. This imperative for change is particularly top of mind for those with marginalized identities like women, first-generation students, and people of color – all identities many of the monologues highlight.

The space given to share these dynamic decision-makers' lived experiences simultaneously demonstrates these women's humility and confidence. They are simple and profound. Invisible and hypervisible. Patient and decisive. They encourage us to "focus on what matters most," "own your gift," "get as much education as you can," and "build[...] things to last that will outlast [you]". They remind us that "I'm only as good as the people I hire," "lived politics are different from perceived politics," "sometimes leadership requires you to look up and out," and that "equity, diversity, and inclusion should be integrated into every operation of the institution." Most importantly they call for us all to remember that regardless of our role, we need to make sure that our students, our communities, and our campus stakeholders "...know every day that they are seen, heard, and valued."

We won't be able to diversify demographics and mindsets that presently predominate higher education leadership without more of the personal, genuine, and multidimensional stories like those of the women in this book who have been trailblazing "firsts" and graciously sharing their authentic stories so that they won't be the last. Their distinct yet parallel stories remind us that one person can make a difference but that if that person wants to stay around, they don't make that difference alone. Through the words of the spotlighted leaders, Takami reminds us of how beautiful, necessary, and cathartic transparency can be. If we want institutions to be open to change and to see and value women as the shrewd decision-makers they are, we have to be willing to embrace every page of their stories – from the lessons learned, to the inextricable link to family, to challenging cultural norms, to paying forward the investment of mentorship, to being unapologetically female, and unapologetically brilliant. Takami puts an emphatic stamp on the fact that these two descriptors never have been and never will be mutually exclusive. In fact, the profiles Takami shares model the possibilities of college and university leadership when individuals leverage the wealth and breadth of their experiences, even if others do not value them.

Raquel M. Rall, Ph.D.
Associate Professor and Faculty Chair,
University of California Riverside School of Education

Women in the Higher Education C-Suite

Women in the Higher Education C-Suite

Diverse Executive Profiles

Lisa Mednick Takami, Ed.D.

Library of Congress Cataloging-in-Publication Data:
Names: Takami, Lisa Mednick, interviewer.
Title: Women in the Higher Education C-Suite: Diverse Executive Profiles
Description: Hoboken, N.J. : John Wiley & Sons Inc., 2024. | Includes bibliographical references and index.
Identifiers: LCCN 2023017154 | ISBN 9781394150236 (paperback) | ISBN 9781394150250 (pdf) | ISBN 9781394150243 (epub) | ISBN 9781394150267 (ebook)
Subjects: LCSH: Women college administrators--United States--Interviews. | Women in higher education--United States. | Educational leadership--United States. | Sexism in higher education--United States.
Classification: LCC LB2341 .W5735 2024 | DDC 378.1/11082--dc23/eng/20230526
LC record available at https://lccn.loc.gov/2023017154

Cover Images: See list of credits inside the book
Cover Design: Wiley

Set in 9.5/12.5pt STIXTwoText by Integra Software Services Pvt. Ltd, Pondicherry, India

To the three loves of my life:
Masahiko, Michael, and Sarah

Contents

About the Author

LISA MEDNICK TAKAMI, ED.D. is a leadership consultant, writer, and higher education administrator. She currently serves as Special Project Director at North Orange Continuing Education, the noncredit educational provider of the North Orange Community College District. Dr. Takami has profiled CEOs and senior leaders for the journal *Women in Higher Education* since 2014. She served as COO for a labor-management apprenticeship training institute during the pandemic and has held administrator and faculty positions at several two-year and four-year institutions. Dr. Takami is the author of *American Mind, Japanese Mind; Cross-Cultural Reflections from East and West* and *Chief Diversity Officers in U.S. Higher Education: Impacting the Campus Climate for Diversity*. Takami resides in Southern California with her husband, Masahiko. They have two adult children, Michael and Sarah.

Foreword

Women in the Higher Education C-Suite makes a strong contribution to the field as an outstanding book about eleven amazing women who have emerged as exemplary leaders. Through a collection of interviews and research, author Dr. Lisa Mednick Takami, gives readers a direct lens into the careers, challenges, innovations, and breakthroughs of their individual journeys. The diverse cultural and racial context of these leaders represents a kaleidoscope of experience that converges into a commonality, the viewpoint of women.

I learned early in my own college and university presidencies that *community* is exactly what women leaders strive to create. I think of my journey and see part of me in each chapter of this book. These experienced CEOs tell us how they approached their new positions with grounded values while embracing the delicate balancing act of taking the reins at the right pace. I recall being told that the first year of a presidency is simply a learning experience, but to remember you are still in charge. Learning the institutional culture is critical for success. Avoiding isolation and bringing in all perspectives is the heart of building community.

Similar characteristics are easily drawn among all chapters – women influenced by upbringing, mentors, coaches, and cultural identities. These leaders embrace intentionality in their career paths, share similar moments of vulnerability and strength, push for inclusivity while following the ethos of a passionate focus on improving the lives of students through post-secondary education. The obstacles of leading through a pandemic have made them stronger, wiser, and more resilient. Each emphasizes the lifelong value of good mentors and coaches. From their perspectives, each highlights the importance of emotional intelligence for leaders. They frequently cite the priority of listening to their constituents and standing ready to change direction as needed.

Readers will be encouraged by the values that drive these women, even in their most stressful moments. They speak of the value of continuous improvement through professional development and the art of effective communication. Even at times when the dreaded "imposter syndrome" might emerge, they use that time to be self-reflective and energized toward growth. They remind us that leaders are so busy taking care of others, they can overlook their own self-care, crucial in order to maintain the strength to pursue their dreams and elevate those of their students.

I have coached presidents; those who are most successful adhere to values of these women. As the reader learns of these individual journeys, it becomes clear each followed the calling of the servant leader. They respect the opinions of others, acknowledge historical contexts, balance the intricacies of shifting cultures, and ultimately create legacies for future generations.

Many speak to the necessity of being at the table when critical decisions are made. Each reports that they are known as breaking the glass ceiling when hired as a woman, the first leader of a diverse multicultural or racial background, or both. Bringing these women into the higher education C-Suite role is not the last stop, however, demonstrated by a repeated theme in their bios of the continued need for inclusivity versus just demographic additions.

They are committed to social and economic mobility, telling stories of their families and the concomitant drivers of gender, race and ethnicity. Many emphasize the importance of authentic leadership. We know each of them in a new way by the end of their chapter because they value being present and real in how they lead.

The life stories told in each chapter demonstrate the skill set needed to navigate the rough seas that were previously captained by men, often those who served as their mentors. While most note they were the first women or racially/ethnically diverse leaders at their institutions and organizations, I would also argue they were the best candidates.

Beyond expressing appreciation for all those who have stood by their side providing guidance and support, each is committed to paying it forward. Current and future higher education leaders will add to their own toolbox by embracing what these women and the author are telling us in this book. Each story provides a very transparent and honest look at what women, and especially women of color, face in their careers. Both women and men in higher education, and those in relevant degree programs, would benefit from this book because it indeed pays forward their wisdom. As a former college president, I have no doubt this book will lead future higher education leaders to be inspired, hopeful, and more prepared to embrace the C-Suite roles that await them.

Barbara Gellman-Danley, Ph.D.
President, Higher Learning Commission

Acknowledgments

With any creative or intellectual endeavor, teams rooted in collaboration and collegiality produce optimal results. This book was born of the steadfast collaboration among many. I am extremely grateful to each of the remarkable leaders whose stories are told within these pages. My appreciation extends to these leaders' executive assistants, chiefs of staff, marketing and communications directors, and other team members who helped provide access, schedule interview dates, track chapter draft reviews, and provide liaison for related content items. I would like to acknowledge the invaluable input of colleagues and mentors who reviewed the initial book proposal and provided expert peer review of draft chapters: Dr. Bill Vega, Dr. Kristi Blackburn, Dr. Jésus Treviño, Dr. Kaye Bragg, Dr. Ashley Griffith, and Dr. Jacqueline Sims. I am indebted to the incredible Wiley teams in New Jersey and Chennai, India for bringing the vision of this book to fruition: Executive Editor, Todd Green, Managing Editor, Pascal Raj François, former Wiley Editor, Monica Rogers, Executive Editorial Assistant, Kelly Gomez, Content Operation Manager, Farhana Haseen, Content Specialist, Krithika Shivakumar and the Wiley creative and production teams. Thank you to Mia Ricci via LinkedIn for the introduction to Todd Green. I am profoundly grateful to Dr. Barbara Gellman-Danley for reviewing the entire manuscript and writing the Foreword. Shout out to Kristie and the Starbucks crew in Torrance for serving up oceans of peach tranquility tea. A special remembrance to my Auntie Debbie, for her steadfast support of my writing, and to my cousin of blessed memory, Sam Albert, also a brilliant writer. Paralleling the leaders profiled in these pages, my success is grounded in the family who support and sustain me in all things: My husband, Masahiko, our son and daughter, Michael and Sarah, my parents, Ellie and Jerry Mednick, and my mother-in-law, Yoshiko Takami.

Introduction
Dr. Lisa Mednick Takami, Ed.D.

During the summer of 2020, at the height of the Covid-19 pandemic, I was recruited and accepted a C-suite position in the private industry education sector. With good wishes from my vice president boss and the college's then president, I bid goodbye to cherished colleagues, a middle management role, and the public, higher education institution where I had successfully served for more than five years.

Within a few months of assuming the C-Suite role, I realized I had underestimated the impact of sexism on the work environment. In retrospect, it was difficult to discern the organization's marginalization of women from the outside. Warning signs and organizational history I overlooked at time of hire became salient later such as one woman serving on a 26-member board.

At the time, I believed the organization was invested in my success after hiring their first woman executive. As COO, I was charged with fulfilling the organization's mission and operationalizing its strategic plan on behalf of 2500 students. I could not see then that I had been placed on a Glass Cliff, a term used by several of this book's participants. The Glass Cliff refers to talented women selected for executive leadership positions without being provided the resources-the personnel, budget, and mentoring support necessary to excel in their roles. In the Glass Cliff scenario, these same resources are readily provided to male executive colleagues. I took charge and concluded I had moved too far from my core values grounded in equity, diversity, inclusion, access, and justice, and I made the difficult decision to transition into a new role.

Women in the Higher Education C-Suite: Diverse Executive Profiles, First Edition.
Lisa Mednick Takami.
© 2024 John Wiley & Sons, Inc. Published 2024 by John Wiley & Sons, Inc.

Learning from this chapter in my career trajectory led to the idea for this book. I endeavored to explore the lived experiences, challenges, and triumphs of successful and diverse women higher education C-suite leaders. What could be learned from this remarkable group of women to inform and prepare the next generation of women leaders?

This book builds on a series of executive profile interviews I wrote for the journal, *Women in Higher Education*, published from 2014-2022. With the onset of the pandemic, I determined there would be significant and relevant experiences to be gained from women CEOs and senior leaders all over the country. I set out to explore diverse higher education women executive leaders in large, public universities, small private colleges, public community colleges, HBCUs, and Tribal Colleges. This book extends my dissertation on higher education Chief Diversity Officers published in 2017 for my doctorate from California State University Long Beach's Education Leadership department.

Semi-structured interviews were conducted with nine women CEOs and two cabinet-level senior executives from January-September 2022. The interviews were conducted via telephone or Zoom with the participants' permission to record the interviews for accuracy. Each chapter begins with a biographical snapshot of how I became acquainted with the executive leader. Responses to interview questions are captured in the leaders' words edited for clarity and publication. Chapter notes, citations, and explanation of votes of no-confidence and the Glass Cliff effect provide context for leaders' experiences and topic discussions. Each chapter ends with the reflection, "What Can We Learn?" describing what the reader can glean from the specific leader's experience and career journey to add to their own leadership toolbox.

I am indebted to these high-achieving women for inviting me into their personal and professional experiences leading higher education institutions before and through the Covid-19 pandemic and the 2020 racial reckoning that continues.

Themes that emerged from the interview data include:

- The foundation of leaders' family relationships, aspirations, examples, and values
- The critical role of mentors, sponsors, trusted supporters, and advisors
- The importance of targeted and ongoing professional development
- The importance of building high performing teams and hiring exceptional candidates

- The complexities and uncertainty of leading through the Covid-19 pandemic
- The commitment to improve access and opportunity for underserved students
- The differential treatment of women leaders relative to their male counterparts including racism, sexism, gender inequities, and the Glass Cliff effect
- The significance of emotional intelligence, political savvy, and collaboration in leadership success
- The ability to self-reflect, course-correct, admit mistakes, and communicate apology when needed
- The joy and exhilaration of leading from the higher education C-Suite despite inherent challenges

Through the writing this book, my respect and admiration for these women has only increased. My belief in the complex higher education mission to provide access and opportunity, inform, prepare, and engage tomorrow's citizenry and leaders has deepened.

I am grateful to these women leaders for their time, their patience, and their willingness to share their experiences leading in higher education today: **Dr. Mildred García, Dr. Dena P. Maloney, Dr. Linda Oubré, Dr. Jane Close Conoley, Dr. Judy K. Sakaki, Dr. Katrice Albert, Dr. Becky R. Petitt, Dr. Joanne Li, Dr. Sandra Boham, Dr. Erika Endrijonas, Dr. Javaune Adams-Gaston, and Dr. Barbara Gellman-Danley.**

May the high bar that these women leaders have set serve as models for the women higher education leaders of today and those of tomorrow.

Lisa Mednick Takami, Ed.D.
June, 2023

1

"I Represent Students in all States to Reach their Potential"

Interview with Dr. Mildred García

Chancellor, California State University System

A portion of this chapter originally appeared in *Women in Higher Education* in December 2021.

Dr. Mildred García became the first Latina woman Chancellor of the California State University System on October 1, 2023. She served as President of the American Association of State Colleges and Universities from January 2018 to September 2023. Previously, she served as President of California State University, Fullerton, California State University, Dominguez Hills, and Berkeley Colleges NY and NJ. I became acquainted with Dr. García at an alumni event during her tenure as President of CSU, Dominguez Hills.

Describe your job in one sentence.

I represent the country's regional state colleges and universities that educate the new student majority in America.

You impart passion for making a difference in higher education. How do you encourage others to take a stake in today's underserved students enrolled in undergraduate and graduate programs?

You must be authentic. I recall bell hooks' quote that you must be a little vulnerable and share a bit about yourself for people to understand the lenses you use to see the world. I tell my personal story, my family's story, my nieces' and nephews' stories and how we started from very little to where we are today. People connect, see themselves, and realize that not everyone is born with a silver spoon in their mouth. Everyone can reach their highest potential if they set their mind to it and have mentors.

What were the significant educational and professional steps in your career trajectory?

My mom gave me the best education I could have asked for when she allowed me (at age 14) to get authorization to work in the factory where she and my cousins worked over the summer. I realized I never wanted my family or me to work in a factory again. It was an awakening. Like many first-generation, low-income students, you want to get yourself and others out of poverty. When you go to school and college, your teachers and professors help you to fall in love with education. That was very significant in my life. I had wonderful teachers and mentors along the way who encouraged and saw things in me that I did not see in myself.

You have spent much of your career in California. What impact did your upbringing have on your career path and decision to return to the East Coast as AASCU President?

Growing up in Brooklyn, there were two tenement buildings filled with people from different ethnicities: Italian Americans, African-Americans, Jewish Americans, and Puerto Ricans all living together. We learned and understood diversity from each other. We learned so much about our neighbors' cultures, and they learned about ours. I brought this experience of diversity to California.

I also brought my school trajectory to California. I started at a community college, which was fortunate. More than 50% of Latinos and many African-American and low-income students start at community colleges. That my first language was Spanish and I began at community college was unique for me as it is for so many students today.

Dr. García with Dr. Cynthia Teniente-Matson, President, San Jose State University

My parents were very strict about speaking Spanish at home and learning English at school so I would have the asset of speaking two languages. When I talk to families, I impart the importance of their children learning English, but I also tell them to hold onto their own language because the asset of language will be important to their kids' future. I transferred from community college and continued my path, which led to earning a master's degree and Doctorate of Education in Higher Education Administration from Teachers College, Columbia University NY. I now represent 3.5 million students from so many different backgrounds. Regardless of their income, students from red states and blue states, it does not really matter. I represent students in all states to reach their potential.

How would you describe the transition from serving as a university president to a national public policy advocate?

I was the first Latina woman president in the California State University system, and I am the first Latina president at AASCU and of the six higher education presidential associations. It is about showing that we have a seat at the table. I have the opportunity to use my bully pulpit not only for Latino students, but for all students, particularly the underrepresented.

When you look at the presidential associations today, there are men at the table, and there are also women! It is extremely important that those who come after me see there is a seat at the table for them. This is important for students but also for the country. The country is slowly starting to recognize that if we do not educate those who have been underserved, this country is in trouble.

What opportunities are inherent to your role at AASCU?

Through AASCU, state college and university presidents have the opportunity to share, learn, and speak about challenges and mistakes among peers they trust. That is exciting for me. All our professional development programs help diversify executive leadership: The New Presidents Academy and The Millennial Leadership Institute, now 22 years old, was started by African-American presidents to diversify the presidency. We have 165 leaders who have become presidents.

AASCU also offers the Academy for New Provosts and the Becoming a Provost Academy, among many other programs.

In the four-year public sector, we have more underrepresented people as presidents than in the private sector. To be the voice of public, regional, comprehensive institutions on Capitol Hill is extremely important. Our students' debt is on average $12–16K when they finish a degree, not the $100K of many other institutions. We stake our rightful place on the Hill and in the public so that families understand we are more affordable, we are smaller, and our faculty teach classes rather than teacher assistants.

What mentors and sponsors have had the greatest impact on your professional journey?

My parents have a wonderful saying that I often use in speeches: "The only inheritance a poor family can leave you is a good education." This expression has stayed with me all my life because it rings true. If you have a good education, you can go far in this country. I had teachers and staff at the community college that saw potential in me. I still have a thesaurus in which a professor wrote, "To Millie, a young lady that will go very far" and encouraged me to go on to my four-year degree.

The staff I worked with in Financial Aid made me a peer advisor and put me through professional development training, all of which helped me to grow. Friends who went before me, my dissertation sponsor, all encouraging me to keep going. My dissertation sponsor, Bob Birnbaum, wrote in his book, "To Millie, who will someday be a president." At that point in my life, I thought he was crazy. When I became president of CSU Fullerton, I called him and he said he was wrong [because] "you are on your third presidency!" My sisters and brothers have been fundamental to my success. Family!

What was the most significant challenge you faced in your career and how did you navigate this situation?

I had been President of Berkeley College for four days when 9/11 hit. We lost 11 students and a faculty member's husband. I remember taking a deep breath, getting everyone together in the auditorium and saying: "Let's hold hands. If you pray, pray. We are going to get through this together." There was no playbook for presidents for 9/11, just like with Covid now. The time after 9/11 and the healing—speaking with family members who lost loved ones and the graduations with posthumous degrees—I still get emotional about it. As a president, I had to be compassionate and upbeat and talk about hope—that was the most challenging. I am a spiritual person. It is about taking moments behind closed doors to acknowledge what you are feeling and then going out there to be empathetic, to give people hope, and to help people get through a horrible situation.

What suggestions do you have for readers aspiring to serve as the CEO of a college, university, or national public policy agency?

Continue learning. Understand what your North Star is and why you want to do these positions. They are not easy. They may look glamorous—they are not. Do the job you are doing well, and other people will recognize you and help you to move forward. Have mentors. Susan L. Taylor (1993) writes in her book, *In the Spirit* that in the front row of your Theater of Life should be people who are encouraging you, applauding you, and helping you along the way.

Author's Note: An updated interview took place with Dr. García in April 2022.

Following the murders of George Floyd, Breonna Taylor, and Ahmaud Arbery and the racial reckoning of 2020, how did the AASCU respond to the #BlackLivesMatter #StopAsianHate, and #MeToo movements?

Of course, like everyone else, we sent out statements. More importantly, and despite Covid, we launched webinars and sprint calls for presidents to discuss with each other and with us what was going on and how to move forward. These efforts were critically important.

Many presidents were seeking promising practices on how to do the transformational work on their campuses. We began to bring in people who had experience and had conducted research. Dr. Frank Harris and Dr. J. Luke Wood, then both at San Diego State University, did a webinar on "Creating an Environment of Racial Justice on Campus". They highlighted not only how to work through the history of each institution and educate the campus, but also how to move forward and implement a 10-point plan they had developed to combat racism.

We brought in Frederick M. Lawrence, an expert on free speech and bias crimes, who gave a webinar on navigating hate speech. We had presidents engaged in conversation about how to discuss the difference between criminal speech and hate speech for those coming from campuses that had been impacted by this issue. We also discussed how to take care of the people hurt by these types of statements. We talk about free speech, but we tend to forget to talk about how we take care of people hurt by free expression.

We also worked with campuses on issues of Anti-Asian Hate and DACA issues. We must not stop talking about these issues. At every conference, we discuss them and how our institutions are doing the systemic, transformational work. We have hosted many experts including Dr. Ibram X. Kendi, Dr. Michael Eric Dyson, and others. Presidents benefit from hearing from these experts, but what they love the most is learning from one another. For example, we just had a seminar where provosts from minority-serving institutions discussed the bomb threats made at HBCUs and violent acts of Anti-Asian hate witnessed in these communities. In short, the AASCU continually works to address these topics.

We have started the process of making all this good work available on our website in the form of white papers and other publications.

What programs and events is the AASCU sponsoring to assist college and university presidents with the return to in-person instruction and work?

At the pandemic's outset, Dr. Michael T. Osterholm, the expert epidemiologist from the University of Minnesota, did a webinar on defining Covid-19 and the extent to which institutions would need to guard against virus spread. This was extremely important for us.

At annual meetings and seminars, we partner with Spartan Medical on protocols for in-person meetings. We had our in-person conference in November 2021. By teaming with Spartan, we demonstrated to presidents how to bring people back. We created our own bubble, tested everyone, and required vaccination status verification. I'm happy to say we had no incidents of Covid among our presidents.

We have continued to conduct webinars on topics such as "How to Open a Campus" and "A Tale of Two Systems". For the latter, we had the heads of Arkansas State University and the California State University systems discuss how they were reopening. We delved carefully into the detailed plans for reopening campuses to students, faculty, and staff. The contrasting system responses proved fascinating. In another webinar, "Return of Athletes in the Age of Covid-19", the President of the NCAA spoke with AASCU presidents of Division 1, Division 2, and Division 3 institutions.

How has the experience of the pandemic impacted your leadership style and AASCU operations moving forward?

My compassion for what people are going through has deepened. Wherever I have worked, I have told my teams, "Family comes first". This time it was different because I usually do surveys and ask people how they are doing, but we were online. In staff meetings, I would ask, "How are you dealing with Covid?", and each person would share. We also had discussions on what people were doing during Covid and how to take care of self, family, children, pets, elderly parents, et. al.

We thought about staff first. We didn't come back until February 22, 2022 because we determined we could help our presidents and their teams by working extremely hard virtually. We developed safety protocols and began by only having staff come back two days per week, so the whole team is not all in the office at the same time. The vice presidents and I go in three times a week. One thing I've always done is to ask, "How are you doing? Is there anything we should know?"

Returning is not only about coming back into the office to work, but also about commutes by public transportation in urban places like Washington, D.C. where AASCU is based. We maintain flexible scheduling and give out test kits at work. Last week, for example, we had some staff attend one of our in-person seminars; afterwards, someone in attendance tested positive. I encouraged the team to test, and in the spirit of caution, we opted not to come into the office the following Monday through Wednesday, worked from home, and everyone was fine. We remain flexible, understanding, compassionate, and careful about safety as a reflection of care for the people we work with. The only way we can get the work done is if everyone is content and morale is high.

[*The author asked Dr. Garcia if she believes teams are honest with her about where they're coming from and referenced Dr. Brené Brown's distinction between hybrid versus flexible work schedules[1] Dr. Garcia indicated one of her vice presidents is trained in Brené Brown's "Dare to Lead"™ work and has conducted "Dare to Lead"™ training at one of the AASCU's member campuses. Dr. Garcia emphasized that she role models with her vice presidents to create a climate where they're comfortable coming to tell her things so that the vice presidents model similarly with their teams.*]

One of our vice presidents is a trained "Dare to Lead"™ facilitator. She's wonderful. I would say she's a Brené Brown groupie. I allow the role modeling that people can tell me what they're feeling. Some people say they're happy to be back in the office because they were tired of being at home all the time; they like the hybrid model so they can be home sometimes, come into work sometimes, and "get the best of both worlds," as one person said to me. I think staff are telling me the truth when they indicate they like the two days working in the office.

[*The author also referenced a discussion with a campus president whose story does not appear in this text. The campus in question has many employees working five days a week. The president of this campus cited a major morale issue among some employee groups. Dr. Garcia continued below.*]

I'm in a different position than campus presidents. In fairness to the presidents who are running campuses, the truth is they have such a complicated team of staff. Presidents must be very careful about the equity issue around campus work. Maintenance, campus police, and employees in areas like IT may have to come in every day no matter what. Considering some of these workers may be low-wage employees and/or people of color, it's difficult for campuses to manage this new reality. Presidents don't want to create a situation of "have's and have not's" where some get to work from home and others need to come in every day impacting those on the front lines when virus transmission numbers are high.

Author's Note: In July 2023, Dr. García was named Chancellor of the California State University System, the nation's largest state university system serving nearly 500,000 students each year. Dr. García discusses her appointment below.[2]

Why and how did you pursue the role of the CSU Chancellor?

I was nominated by multiple individuals in the field. I was not seeking this position because I am also passionate about my work at AASCU and the advocacy for the institutions we serve. At AASCU, we help to diversify senior administrators, particularly presidents and chancellors. What convinced me [to pursue and accept this role] was a dedicated board, presidents, faculty, staff, administrators, and students completely committed to student success, especially for those underserved. The CSUs serve almost a half million students and last year alone conferred degrees to 120,000 students.

What do you see as the significance of your appointment as the first Latina woman to hold this role?

I see myself opening doors for other Latinas and women of color to reach their highest potential. While I am honored and humbled, it is a sad statement that I am the first in the 21st century. Hopefully, we will see many more women of color in the higher echelons of postsecondary education.

What would you like your legacy to be?

I would like my legacy to be that I cared about people who were underserved and underrepresented.

I'm in this business because I want people to reach their highest potential regardless of background. I have a lot to be thankful for. My public education system (New York City public schools) gave me the foundation, but I had a guidance counselor once tell me I would never go to college ... and here I am. I want everyone to "have their shot" to reach their highest potential regardless of socioeconomic background, race, religion, immigration status, ability status, ethnicity, gender, sexuality, or other social identities. Those of us who are fortunate to go through the doors of higher education to shatter ceilings have an obligation to continue to bring others through those same doors to shatter other ceilings.

What Can We Learn?

Dr. García highlights remaining genuine in how we support students' greatest aspirations to reach their highest potential by also supporting one another in the workplace. She references lessons from her family upbringing and schooling- being immersed in diverse communities, committing to bringing her family out of poverty, being guided by key advisors and mentors-as central to her leadership approach and success as the first female Latina leader in multiple higher education executive roles.

Notes

1 Brown, B. & Guillen, B. (Hosts). (2022, May 9) Brené and Barrett on gathering together for the first time [audio podcast episode] in *Dare to lead*. Spotify.

2 The California State University. (2023, July 12). *Mildred García appointed 11th CSU Chancellor*. [Press Release] https://www.calstate.edu/csu-system/news/Pages/CSU-11th-Chancellor-Appointed-2023.aspx.

2

"It Matters Who Is in the Room"

Interview with Dr. Linda Oubré

President Emeritus, Whittier College

Dr. Linda Oubré was appointed President of Whittier College, California in July 2018. I became acquainted with Dr. Oubré through her participation in the Black Student Success Week in April 2021, sponsored by the California Community Colleges. Dr. Oubré retired as President of Whittier College at the end of June 2023. She was named President Emeritus in recognition of her strong leadership and role as a change maker at Whittier. Dr. Oubré plans to continue to work on causes that advance diversity, equity, inclusion, social justice, and access to higher education for all.

A portion of this chapter originally appeared in *Women in Higher Education* in August 2021.

Describe your job in one sentence:

I am developing the diverse pipeline of future leaders who will change the world.

Women in the Higher Education C-Suite: Diverse Executive Profiles, First Edition.
Lisa Mednick Takami.
© 2024 John Wiley & Sons, Inc. Published 2024 by John Wiley & Sons, Inc.

Your professional path to the presidency was atypical. Please share the significant educational and professional steps in your career trajectory.

I have always had an interest in education. I went to Hollywood High and UCLA, the first person in my family to go to college directly from high school. I wanted to be a journalist, but I was good in math, so I majored in economics. I was admitted to the Harvard Business School MBA program after working for a commercial bank for two years. It was a culture shock, but it was also the best thing I've ever done. For a year, I was Director of Admissions for the Harvard MBA program. Demystifying the school to attract diverse students was much of the job.

I worked for the *Los Angeles Times* in financial planning and got recruited to Disney when they were starting their publishing division. I began consulting, met a billionaire who had an idea and started a company which went public and allowed me to help retire and start teaching. I taught at Wharton at the University of Pennsylvania, UC Davis, San Diego State University and then returned to UC Davis doing corporate relations in 2011.

Business schools were starting to recognize they needed businesspeople to teach and run the school. I ran industry relations, the part-time MBA program, and served as the business school's chief diversity officer. After a year and a half, San Francisco State University (SFSU) sought a business dean. I spent six years at SFSU. Building corporate relations was much of the job. My provost said I should get a doctorate to become a president, so I got my doctorate at the University of Pennsylvania.

After the first year, I started getting calls about president roles. Whittier College is a very diverse campus. The college was looking for someone innovative and entrepreneurial, a diverse candidate who understood Los Angeles' unique multiculturalism and had a business and higher education background. My business background is important in higher ed, especially post-COVID.

How would you describe your leadership style and approach?

I always hire people better than me. Many leaders get threatened by people. I really like a strong team who are better at things [that] I'm not as good at. I hire people who wear a lot of different hats. In a small college, this is helpful because they weigh in on many different things.

I like data and metrics, and I expect my team to like data and metrics. Give me an idea of what the investment is [and] what the return is. I'm

also extremely people oriented. I get to know every individual, what motivates them...as opposed to a blanket way of managing people.

I'm only as good as the people I hire.

Students of color constitute 69% of Whittier's student body, making it one of the most diverse private liberal arts colleges in the country. As a transformational leader, what steps did you take to diversify college leadership?[1]

It matters who is in the room. At my first Cabinet meeting, there were all men, mostly white, except the executive assistant. The conversation was about who was going to which game or who was playing golf with whom. I immediately redefined what "Cabinet" meant. I added the human resources person, who's a Black woman. I promoted the Communications, HR, and Development Directors, all three women. The faculty chair wasn't in the room because the previous administration didn't agree with them and hadn't invited them. That person is a transgender man and I invited them.

The conversations changed in the second meeting to topics...to drive the organization forward. By the end of my first year, all the men except the CFO had left. Each time someone left, it allowed me to recruit and bring in more diverse leaders. When someone who looks like me manages the college, it brings in more diverse applicants.

What are some of the inherent challenges and opportunities in serving as President of Whittier College and as its first president of color?

At any college, true equity and inclusion takes hard work. I stepped into an institution that was diverse by the numbers, but our student populations did not feel there was a welcoming environment. The best example was Dr. Martin Luther King Jr. Day last year. The Black students started a petition because we did not honor the holiday. There were only two institutions in California that did not celebrate the holiday. When a reporter called, he wanted to write about Richard Nixon's alma mater not celebrating the holiday. I let him know I had supported the Black students' petition. Now the college recognizes MLK Day and César Chavez Day.

The benefit of diverse leadership is we have lived the experiences of diverse students. Only about 11% of private colleges' board members are people of color. Yet, women students are the highest demographic group in colleges, and students of color are the growing group, just under half of all college students. We're diversifying our Board of Trustees. Trustees at most small, private colleges are alumni who attended the school a long time ago. Many of our trustees attended Whittier College when Richard Nixon was president because he was president and a Whittier alum. We recently had a meeting and added three more board members. Higher ed must tackle diversifying the board because they're the institution's true leaders and...need to represent the students they're serving.

Institutions need trustees with different backgrounds. I've added people who are not alums to the board because we need different viewpoints based on diversity of age, ethnicity, socioeconomic status, and gender.

What impact did your family and upbringing have on your career path?

My mother is my role model. She quit high school to get married and moved from Detroit to L.A. and was divorced with five kids by the time she was 24. Speed forward and she had an MBA and five Emmy Awards, and she'd married my stepfather, who was a UCLA administrator. My grandparents always told us, "Get as much education as you can stand because it's the only thing someone can't take away from you." They were civil rights and union rights activists. My grandparents were a really strong influence on me.

What mentors/sponsors have had the greatest impact on your professional journey?

A woman business leader related this analogy: You need a personal board of directors. I've taken this approach to heart. There are people I go to when I want to talk through marketing issues and others I go to for career or personal things. Especially as women and people of color, you must find several people. Having the credentials and education I obtained was probably the most important factor. I've had sponsors because of those credentials and alumni networks.

What knowledge, skills and abilities would you recommend to readers interested in pursuing a CEO role in higher education?

Higher education is a business model. Take classes in finance, financial planning, marketing, strategic planning, and understand economics. If you come up the academic side, get experiences managing people, but make sure to take courses like finance in higher ed and marketing. Career-wise, try something different, e.g., volunteer for the strategic planning task force...or launch a certificate program to show you're entrepreneurial. People tend to be afraid of fundraising, but they shouldn't be. It's about saying, "I have a great idea and...I can talk to you about it and ask you to fund it!"

We must be innovative as presidents.

Author's Note: An updated interview was conducted with Dr. Oubré in April 2022.

What are your 2022 leadership priorities at Whittier College?

The biggest thing is trying to recreate and reinvent ourselves. The business model for small colleges was broken before Covid. This has been a very challenging environment for small colleges. At Whittier, my board, my leadership team, and I see this as an opportunity to recreate the future and do something different. Much of what we have been working on is putting in place foundations for the future. The business model was broken for colleges for different reasons including demographic shifts; we must find ways to educate new markets of students.

That means more diverse students, more first-generation students, more LatinX students, and a declining market of high school graduates.

The world is changing so fast that people will look for education throughout their lifetime instead of getting a degree and using that degree at one company for 40 years. We are talking about ways that we can look at the entire life cycle of learning and we aim to be more accessible for all types of students. A big part of this is embracing who we are at Whittier and who we have become. Except for Spelman College, there are no institutions that can say we educate women of color. Women of color are our best students in terms of retention and graduation rates, something we need to start celebrating!

In California, a third of the population is women of color, and that includes children, but they are our future. We must continue to be very strong with that population. We are really working on re-focusing, which means our student may be a single mom in her 30's who has come back to get her degree, or someone who already has a degree and wants to start a new career. This means providing education in new and different ways and providing varied delivery methods. We learned a lot from Covid and having to go remote in two weeks. We did a pretty good job. I say "remote" rather than "online" because we are thinking beyond online; we are thinking about how to deliver education in a different way that utilizes technology. Technology is here to stay, forever-changing and brings together all students, not just traditional students. We also want to bring students to campus for high-impact learning experiences like experiential learning. We are trying to do something different.

I use the word "celebrate". Diversity is not new to Whittier. We have been doing a great job with these populations for the last decade, but we never talked about it. We are going to start talking about it. By talking about diversity, equity, and inclusion, we have started talking about why these populations are important, but we will continue to talk about it and celebrate it! Whittier has been around for 130 years; it is going to take more than a few years to change the culture and the image. If you have not heard it yet, you will. This is part of the planning. I just had my board retreat last weekend and have been getting buy-in from the board on all of these plans.

Whittier would have never received $12 million from Mackenzie Scott[2] if we were not already talking about these populations, what we are doing for students, and how we are changing the culture of Whittier College. In terms of campaigns, a few years ago we started the quiet phase of the first campaign not focused on capital but focusing on student success. Student success is equity, diversity, and inclusion, which attracted the Mackenzie Scott money and other foundation money. One of the key things is that we are also looking for corporate money and corporate industry partners that are interested in employees who look like our students. We are really starting to build these partnerships.

Many of my alums and donors think I am talking about the changing face of Whittier too much, so they notice, but it is simple marketing and branding. I always tell my team that you have to remember that I used to work for a company that has convinced the world to buy things with the face of a mouse on them (Disney). Essentially, Mickey is this mouse, and here is this company that has invested billions of dollars into making a mouse cute and cuddly and something that people want.

I believe that you can brand almost anything, but it is also vision. If you were to look at our marketing and communications now versus five years ago, you'd see the types of stories we are doing are different. The fact that we are even talking about Black History Month, the student profiles we highlight, the fact that we now have more diversity in all our materials, and the face of our board and our leadership team that has changed: that is all part of our brand.

You have commented that the pandemic provided opportunity for presidents and institutions to do things differently. How will changes adopted during the pandemic be sustained at Whittier College moving forward?

Using technology is key. Not only did we go remote with our teaching, but since we have been back on campus after going remote during Omicron, students have commented, "I could have done this online,". It is a matter of figuring out what works online and what works in person and using both in combination. Also, in terms of how we do our jobs. I have a great book on my desk, *Remote Work Revolution* (Neeley, 2021);[3] she is at the Harvard Business School and her book is getting a lot of play. We have learned that we do not always need to be in the room to be efficient; this is applicable to work and in the classroom. We have learned that you do not always have to get on an airplane to have meetings with people. We apply this concept in admissions; because we could not be in person during the pandemic, in many ways, our admissions team has continued to have a lot of touch points with prospective students. Zoom offered more one on one time, and it has made us more efficient. You do not have to travel three hours to visit one high school with 100 kids so we use time more efficiently. The same thing with fundraising. In many ways, the pandemic and the use of technology have made us much more efficient. Also, it has made us value more the time we are together and value the time we are in person.

In looking at your career trajectory, what are you most proud of? Is there anything you regret or wish you had done differently?

I am most proud of getting my doctorate at the age of 58 (in 2017) because higher education administration was a third career which I did not have to pursue; I could have been a business dean for the rest of my career. I learned so, so much, and that is what I am most proud of. I think we all wish we may have done some things differently, but everything I have done, mistakes included, is part of who I am. You learn from these things. I have had some really difficult situations as most people have had. I am a strong, resilient person. Even so, I wish I had had the strength to speak up sooner at Whittier about racism that I was experiencing. I spoke up, but I wish I could have been stronger. I wish I would have stood on a table and screamed it instead. I spoke up soon, so it was not timing, but I trusted the powers that be too much.

I am going to steal some advice from Ruth Simmons.[4] I had the pleasure to moderate a panel discussion between Dr. Simmons and Dr. Bob Zemsky, a legend in higher ed, at the University of Pennsylvania's Executive Doctorate Higher Education Management Conference. Dr. Simmons had received the Robert Zemsky Medal for Innovation in Higher Education.

Ruth said something I wish I had done. When she took the job at Brown, her first presidency, she told the board, "You need to understand I'm a Black woman and these are the things I am going to work on including a reckoning of Brown's racist past." Brown was in business with one of the largest slave traders. She indicated this and her other priorities up front and said if the board was not comfortable with this then not to pick her. I thought this was such great advice when I had already been in the job a few years.

When you are hiring someone new and diverse, we are nice, shiny objects, but if organizations and those hiring have never had a diverse experience or the lived experience of a woman or person of color, they do not know what these experiences mean. In the summer of 2021, the Harvard Business School published a case study, *Linda Oubré at Whittier College*, examining how I diversified leadership of the college board.[5] It is a great case, and they invited me to attend the first class that used the case. The students said, "We don't get it, they hired you for diversity." I said, "They didn't hire me because of diversity. They hired me because of the business model I proposed. They hired me because I'm from Los Angeles. They hired me because I was Bob Zemsky's student (Zemsky was also a board member) and because of my higher ed and business background." Frankly, I think they had no idea what it means to hire a woman of color. In their lives, they had no experience working with people who look like me. When I said at Whittier, "We have some problems here; we are diverse, but we are not very equitable or inclusive," they did not know how to handle it because they had no experience addressing these issues.

The Harvard Case Study was written during a difficult time. I had board members leave because they were not on board with the new vision. Going to Harvard was surreal. My husband came with me; he's also a Harvard MBA.

If you were to design a higher education doctoral program, what courses would you prioritize for future leaders?

Bob Zemsky designed the executive higher education management doctoral program at Penn. At my board retreat, I had the pleasure of bringing Dr. Peter Eckel, one of my professors who does governance and higher ed leadership, and Dr. Shaun Harper, founder and executive director of USC's Race and Equity Center, to present. In doctoral programs, they talk about governance and managing boards, but this is the toughest area. They talk about the context of shared governance, but I told Peter he needs to share my Harvard Business Case Study with classes going forward; they didn't spend enough time on the topic of working with and managing boards. I went to the Penn Exec Doc program which covers everything. There is a reason there are more graduates that have presidencies from that doctoral program than from any other; it really is a great survey program. People ask me how my job is different from that of a dean. The one area I did not manage as a dean was athletics, so perhaps an athletics course would be a good addition.

What Can We Learn?

Dr. Oubré's story demonstrates that a private sector career and a background in finance can provide an excellent foundation for higher education executive roles. Many skills are transferable between sectors, and an understanding of budgets, funding streams, and operations is critical in today's higher education environment where presidents are expected to have fund development savvy. Dr. Oubré shares her personal journey in navigating racism, the importance of speaking up quickly and broadly, and the need to communicate one's leadership priorities when entering a role not previously held by a person of color.

Notes

1 Whittier College. (2022). *Facts and Figures.* https://www.whittier.edu/about/facts.

2 Whittier College. (2021, March 17). *Scott gift transforming Whittier College.* https://www.whittier.edu/news/wed-03172021-1001-am/scott-gift-transforming-whittier-college.

3 Neeley, T. (2021). *Remote work revolution: Succeeding from anywhere.* New York: HarperCollins.

4 Dr. Ruth Simmons served as the 18th president of Brown University and currently serves as professor at Prairie View A&M University, an HBCU, after having served as its president.

5 Spar, D.L., & Brown, H.P. (2021). *Linda Oubré at Whittier College.* Harvard Business School. https://store.hbr.org/product/linda-oubre-at-whittier-college/721057.

3

"Leadership Is Really an Orientation Toward Action"

Interview with Dr. Dena P. Maloney

Retired Superintendent/President, El Camino Community College District

A portion of this chapter originally appeared in *Women in Higher Education* in September 2016.

Dr. Dena P. Maloney became the first woman Superintendent/President of the El Camino Community College District in Torrance, California where she began her tenure in February 2016. I became acquainted with Dr. Maloney through my work managing the professional development and learning department at El Camino College. Prior to El Camino College, Dr. Maloney served with distinction as Superintendent/President of the West Kern Community College District/ Taft College from 2012 to 2015. Dr. Maloney retired from higher education in June 2021.

Describe your job in one sentence.

I'm an educational leader and a collaborator and I have to set the environment for the college to have the creativity and innovation it requires to respond to the needs of students. As leaders, we have to be very genuinely enthusiastic about what we're doing and who we're serving. We need to create systems that support delivering on our mission to our students and our communities.

What is the role of these "systems"?

Systems are not only the organizational structures that enable us to support student learning, but also the communication systems, the collaboration systems, the cross-functional teams that might be needed to start something new.

Systems have to be established, maintained and evaluated to see if they're working and what else is needed to bring this whole enterprise, this academy, this institution together to function effectively and produce the outcomes we're seeking for students to achieve their goals.

There's an inherent decency to your leadership approach. Who or what has been significant in influencing your leadership style?

I often talk about my mother as my role model. My mother is an amazing person. She instilled in me the values of commitment, dedication, and the willingness to work hard. My mother was the Camp Fire Girls leader and the PTA president.

Much of what I did growing up had to do with giving service, always being aware that there are those who need more than you do and that you are blessed to be able to contribute to others. My mother and father shaped who I am as a person and therefore how I view leadership.

What do you see as the connection between this ethos of service and your pursuit of leadership?

Leadership is really an orientation toward action in the service of some goal or some group. From my mother, I can remember my Camp Fire Girl troop going and being in convalescent homes and entertaining the patients by singing. My mother helped us to see that serving others is a privilege.

There's a whole body of literature and theory about servant leadership, and in the context of my upbringing, this is where my leadership perspective falls.

You discuss the notion of "leading from where you are." Describe what you mean and how women in higher education might learn from your example.

We all have the opportunity to positively influence those around us in our work setting. When we truly own our work and we take responsibility for solving operational problems or improving what we do, we're exercising leadership. Leadership really stems from a state of mind rather than—although it's important sometimes—a position of authority.

You can lead from wherever you are if you have the mindset of being accountable and responsible for your work and helping your team. The other component needed is an *environment* that supports "leading from where you are." Absent the environment, this orientation would be difficult and could lead to frustration, resulting in employees "checking out" or moving on to a new opportunity elsewhere.

You're a first-generation student. How does your educational journey impact your role as a community college president?

As a first-generation college student, I have an appreciation for the challenges that come from not having role models who have navigated higher education.

In high school, I remember not being clear on my goals and believing I had to know what I wanted to become to go to college. That was the thinking at the time; you go to college because you want to be an engineer, or you go to college because you want to be a nurse. I decided to attend a community college, and it's the best thing I ever did!

In a community college environment where knowledge and studying were valued, I realized I didn't have to know exactly what I wanted to become, but rather what I wanted to study.

Within that first year, I applied for and got a scholarship and transferred, but I was always thankful that I had that first year at a community college. I went on and earned a bachelor's and a master's degree and ultimately a doctorate. My experience as a first gen student instilled in me an appreciation for the first gen students throughout our community college system. I drew upon my own experiences in supporting students throughout my tenure in higher education.

We all have the capacity as staff, administrators, or faculty to help students who don't have clear-cut goals to get through that first year. El Camino's campus community has a long tradition of helping students persist and achieve their goals.

What was your educational and career path leading to your appointment as El Camino College's superintendent/president?

My career path followed the economic workforce and development route, which is not typical for college presidents. After I got my master's degree in government, I went to work in the private sector and then I joined the College of the Canyons in Santa Clarita, California.

My first position was to link the community college with the surrounding business community. In the course of that first position, I came to know more deeply the mission of the California Community Colleges, which I embraced.

I found the college to be a very exciting and invigorating environment in which to work. After serving as the dean of economic and workforce development and earning my doctoral degree in educational leadership, I was selected to be the founding dean of the Canyon Country Campus. This new position took me out of the economic and workforce development niche and helped to broaden my scope of responsibilities.

I led a team that was starting a brand-new campus and helped develop its spirit and culture. From there, I became the superintendent/president at Taft College in the Central Valley. Taft is a small, rural college with an economic environment and industry base different from where I'd been. Then, I came to El Camino. My background has prepared me well to serve at El Camino College. We're situated in a very diverse economy and community where my strengths in economic and workforce development can be leveraged. My progression has been different from the path of a traditional presidency, but more and more, the kinds of experiences needed of a president are changing. Often presidents are the chief fundraiser, chief advancement officer and chief relationship-builder for their institution.

You are an inclusive leader. How do you impart your approach to leadership to other campus leaders?

My approach to leadership is self-evident. I model the kind of behavior and actions I expect the leadership team to adopt and provide opportunities for leaders to develop their skills and facilitate team development. Recently, we undertook a management training program called "Partnership Forward" to help our leadership team understand each other in the context of working as partners to design the future of the institution.

Professional development is a critical function in any organization. People need to be armed with the skills, knowledge and experiences that will help them contribute fully to the institution. There's a clear link between professional development and the health of the college in such areas as enrollment. We need to have the opportunity to develop ourselves professionally and move the college forward.

Approximately 46% percent of CEOs in the California Community Colleges System are women versus the 32% higher education national average. How do you explain this better success rate in California?[1]

California's diversity has helped the success of women leaders. Because women have attained leadership positions as CEOs in the community college system, they've been visionary in creating professional development programs.

Many opportunities exist to develop professionally. One is the Asilomar Leadership Skills Seminar. Dr. Dianne G. Van Hook, a wonderful mentor, recommended that I attend and indicated that I had the potential to be a college president. I will always be indebted to Dr. Van Hook for her unwavering confidence in me.

One of the things I picked up on from women CEOs who spoke at Asilomar was the joy they had for their work. The Association of California Community College Administrators also has a mentor program to help develop women (and men) leaders. Dr. Nicki Harrington became my mentor. She suggested I review job announcements for presidential positions to identify gaps in my experience and then seek opportunities to develop expertise in these areas. This was invaluable advice.

What would you like to accomplish during your tenure at El Camino College?

I would like to continue the great tradition that El Camino College has in academic and learning support programs that help students achieve their goals with equitable outcomes. I hope that we can become even more engaged with our community and the campus culture evolves so that we have innovation and creativity to a greater extent than perhaps we can even envision right now.

The world around us is changing so much. Institutions need to be flexible and adaptable and embrace change.

Author's Note: Dr. Maloney retired in July 2021. An updated interview took place with her in February 2022.

Looking back at your career trajectory, what are you most proud of, and is there anything you wish you had done differently?

I am very proud that in every place I worked, I tried to help people more broadly understand the college, what it stands for, and how it how it helps the community, employees, and students.

Earlier in my career, in about 2000, I do not think people understood that the California Community College system had economic and workforce development (EWD) as part of its mission; EWD was the least understood function of the college. At College of the Canyons, where I served as a founding dean and a vice president, I felt that conditions were ripe for that part of our mission to be more prominent. In so doing, the benefit is not only to companies and employees that colleges may be working with, but also to students.

Much of what we learned working with businesses made its way into academic programs. I am proud that during that time in my career, I played a role in this development. Now, there is a far different understanding; community colleges *are* seen as a key driver in building workforce capacity. Especially at this time with the pandemic, talent development is so important, and community colleges are positioned to help economic and workforce development move forward through academic programs and other services. During my career, I had the chance to put EWD into practice and see it unfold locally, regionally, and at the state level. I am really proud of that!

In terms of broadening the institution, a second thing I am proud of is the PRIDE leadership and mentoring academies established at El Camino College. (PRIDE stands for the college's values, People, Respect, Integrity, Diversity, Excellence). At El Camino, there had not been a focus on internally developing leaders prior to my arrival. There was not a structured process where people could learn how they could play a role whether or not they were a manager, a faculty member, or a classified staff member. Everybody had their niche. As the CEO, I recognized my responsibility to tap into the vast array of talent at the institution. I felt it was important for employees to understand that I welcomed their engagement and involvement with their ideas and energy. I coined the phrase to "lead from where you are" to help make the college a better place. The ECC PRIDE program was really important and ignited energy within the college.

I selected a design team which designed the program content and an application process for potential participants to be admitted into the program over a period of months. The "design team model" is now being used in the Academic Senate for its equity development training. While the PRIDE program may change over time, the structure of how to create these programs and offer them to the college is embedded, and I am excited about that. The design team concept is critical, and there is something to be said about urgency; we had to pull our ideas together quickly, which unleashed a lot of creativity. It worked very well for El Camino College. I am so proud of that program. People really enjoyed themselves and grew their skills through the program, which makes me very proud.[2]

Under the same umbrella of broadening institutional change and understanding at El Camino College is the South Bay Promise Program. The program started as a way to access higher education for a small number of students from selected local high schools. Their enrollment fees were waived as a result of their participation. However, in working with a team of ECC employees, we re-envisioned the program to be not only about access, but also about *success*. Access to higher education alone does not constitute success. The goal is success. To reach success, these students need support! The program tied in beautifully with other institutional initiatives, such as the Starfish Early Alert platform, known as ECC Connect. The transformation of the South Bay Promise program broadened the institution's understanding of its mission and what it represents to students.

In terms of things I may have done differently, we cannot underestimate the importance of communication. During the pandemic, when we had to turn on a dime, it chipped away at one of the strengths I have as a leader, which is connecting with people. Working in a remote campus operations environment was so challenging. Communication suffered, and I was not able to connect with our employees in the manner that leveraged my communication skills. As leaders, we must be prepared for all kinds of things and ensure our skills are ready for challenges–but the remote environment really threw me for a loop. It was a very hard time for the institution and for me as a leader to feel that I was communicating and making an impact. In times of crisis, you don't want to make rash decisions that you need to apologize for later.

A sensitive matter was the projected deficit of the state budget, expected to be $56 billion in May 2020. In response, the College instituted management furloughs. If we had been in a room together and had talked about the budget problems we faced, maybe somebody would have come up with an even better idea. However, when you get into that "hunkered down" feeling, you can make decisions that are not always the best reasoned. Not engaging the people impacted by a decision compromises the decision and those affected by it.

I could have avoided this scenario if I had thought about it better. I began to see how the pandemic was affecting my leadership skill set in communications. Ultimately, it came down to my reflecting on the action I took, the impact it had, and the damage to the group that was not intended. I apologized for the way in which the decision had been made. I thought it was important to reopen the conversation with a team of people I trusted, looked to, and respected in order to share my thoughts. That is what leaders do; they reflect on their decisions and take ownership. If people are going to share their feedback with you, to not respond shows a lack of respect. You must reflect and feel your way through these difficult decisions. Leaders are not perfect. At the end of the day, give people the respect they deserve by showing that you care. You may not have the answer they are looking for, but you must show that you heard them.

You attended the Asilomar Institute before you became a CEO, and during your tenure at El Camino College, you served as a Wheelhouse Fellow. What role do you believe professional development should play for women higher education leaders?

Professional development is essential. To ignore one's own development and learning is a big mistake. No matter how much you prepare for a presidency, even if through the traditional route of student services or academic affairs, you have to know enough about every aspect of the college to hold managers leading those areas accountable and make sure things are moving in the right direction.

Professional development is important in ways different than what we would think. At the CEO level, the learning from fellow CEOs and the peer relationships that you develop are critical so that you can pick up the phone and ask a peer about something that you may not know anything about. You must be willing to be vulnerable with your peers and rely on them to get information to fill a gap in your own expertise. Beyond a technical understanding, college CEOs must have a knowledge of leadership itself. You must understand finance and student success, but you also have to understand organizational culture, how to lead change, and move the organization forward. Bringing in some outside expertise is really important for some of these areas. The Asilomar Institute and the Wheelhouse Fellowship really helped me to understand what it takes to be a leader and an effective CEO, as well as building a network of peers to collaborate with during my tenure as president.

How did the murders of George Floyd, Breonna Taylor, and Ahmaud Arbery and the racial reckoning of 2020 impact you as a leader? How did the college respond?

The murders of George Floyd, Breonna Taylor, and Ahmaud Arbery deeply impacted me both personally and as a leader. The taking of human life, time and again over our history, was deeply disturbing. Particularly in the matter of George Floyd, in which the murder was so callous and deliberate, it was truly shocking. There was a feeling of disbelief, anger, and grief across the nation. But for those who have advocated for racial justice over countless years, sadly there was no sense of disbelief. Murders such as these have been happening for many years.

I realized that as hard as these developments may have been for me, they were immeasurably difficult for those who are Black or African American, already deeply engaged in the work of racial and social justice. Words of wisdom or comfort from me seemed inadequate and hollow in the face of such a grievous affront to humanity. Yet I knew that the campus community rightly expected a statement from me, as the college president, to make a statement that acknowledged the grief, outrage, sadness and anger felt by the college community. It took some time to pull my thoughts together and issue a statement acknowledging the injustice of these murders, and sharing my own sense of grief and anger with the campus.

The months that followed was a period of growth and awareness for me as leader of the college and my own experiences as a white woman in America. I personally became more aware of the different ways members of the campus community experienced El Camino College. Students, faculty, and staff shared in various campus conversations their experiences of racism, microaggressions, and the absence of equitable practices on campus. Painful as it was, this period was a time of growth at our college through conversations and dialogue about the issues facing our institution within the wider context of race relations in America.

Perhaps most helpful to me at this time were conversations with members of the African American Employees Network (AFAM) at El Camino. Their ideas and suggestions, both wide ranging and sweeping, helped me as a leader start to conceptualize the level and scope of organizational change necessary to improve racial relations and equity on our campus.

In the 2020–21 academic year, the college put into motion numerous initiatives to support diversity, equity and inclusion on our campus. Some initiatives were already underway prior to the events of May 26, 2020, but the focus and intensity of these efforts were heightened. These initiatives were led by faculty, classified staff, administrators, and students. The college joined the USC Race and Equity program and asked for interested members of the campus community to attend monthly sessions through the program. There was a positive response to the call for participation and each session included faculty, staff and students who shared their learning in campus discussions following each session. The college's SITE (Scholarly Inquiry in Teaching Excellence) committee, a faculty-led group focused on ensuring El Camino College is actively anti-racist, facilitated these campus discussions.

The El Camino College Academic Senate adopted a resolution in support of anti-racism and equity and launched an effort to create a Faculty Development Program focused on anti-racist teaching practices. The college also established a President's Advisory Committee on Race and Equity which developed recommendations in support of anti-racism and student equity. The Advisory Committee, which included members of all campus constituents, produced a student-led recommendation to establish a Social Justice Center on campus. The Board of Trustees created a board committee to examine board policies and update them to reflect the district's commitment to diversity, equity and inclusion. Among the most active campus groups, the aforementioned El Camino College African American Employees Network (AFAM) facilitated discussions, supported campus-wide teaching moments, and served as an important voice in campus conversations regarding race.

The challenges that faced our campus in light of the George Floyd, Breonna Taylor, and Ahmaud Arbery murders are real. The pain of these events is real. As a leader, I wanted to help our campus community heal. However, I recognized that pain and anguish this deep takes shared leadership at all levels, working through the many challenges we face. Institutional practices are not easy to change. Our collective commitment to the goal of creating a racially just, positive campus culture, the willingness to tackle difficult issues, is the foundation for organizational change at El Camino College.

What prompted you to retire in 2021?

Retiring was part of a larger life plan that my husband and I developed over the years. When I was selected as the Superintendent/President of the El Camino College District, the board[3] asked me about my career trajectory, and I indicated that I planned to stay a minimum of five years. The board was comfortable with this and saw me as someone new coming in after a long period of stable leadership.[4] In organizational change theory, there is the concept of unfreezing the status quo, and I saw my role as unfreezing the status quo.[5] As excellent as previous leadership may have been, the very fact that the institution has a *new leader* in that role constitutes change. I was very intentional about what I wanted to accomplish in the five years that I served at the college: Working with the CEO of the Compton Community College District to complete our partnership with Compton College successfully; continuing the capital construction building program to modernize the El Camino College campus; expanding the South Bay Promise; and growing the talent within the college.

I had a chart of goals for each year, and I followed it. By the time I was ready to talk to the board about retirement, I felt we had made good progress on many of those goals.

In the last three years, my son and daughter have gotten married, and we now have two grandchildren. This phase of our lives is about us as a couple, about things we enjoy, and time with friends and family. We relocated and are discovering organizations in our town that we are interested in joining, and this is a big transition time for us. We love it and what we hoped would happen when we retired. I do feel it is all right to set aside something that you have loved so much and worked so hard at for a long time to explore other things at a different stage in life. I think life is more than our professional callings. My husband and I feel so blessed to have this time together.

What would you like your professional legacy to be?

The mission of El Camino College is to make a positive difference in people's lives. This is the reason I aligned so well as a candidate for the CEO job. Wherever I have worked, and wherever I have provided some contribution, I wanted to make a positive difference. Through my service, I had the opportunity to make things better. That is what I want my legacy to be: I have worked at three institutions, and in each of those three, I did my personal best. In each of those three, I wanted to add something unique that would leave the institution better than when I started. This is what I hope my legacy will be.

What Can We Learn?

Dr. Maloney points out that each of us can make an important impact, at any level of the organization, by taking responsibility for our work product, positively influencing those around us, and helping our teams by solving operational problems or improving what we do. She emphasizes the importance of enthusiasm and the critical nature of creating and evaluating systems (communication, collaboration, cross-functional teams) on operationalizing the college's mission and supporting students achieving their educational goals. Dr. Maloney pursued her own professional development (e.g., formal mentoring) and was recommended for professional growth programs which she cites as key to her obtaining two CEO roles.

Notes

1 Fuesting, M., Bischel, J., & Schmidt, A. (2022). *Women in the leadership pipeline in higher education have better representation and pay in institutions with female presidents and provosts.* College and University Professional Association for Human Resources. https://www.cupahr. org/surveys/research-briefs/women-executives-in-higher-ed.

Mize, R., et. al. (2022). *California community college CEO tenure & retention study.* Community College League of California. https:// ccleague.org/sites/default/files/publications/CEO/cclc_ceo-tenure-report_10.2022-v7.pdf.

2 The author chaired the founding design team of the El Camino College PRIDE Leadership Development Academy. In 2020, ECC PRIDE received a commendation from the Accrediting Commission for Community and Junior Colleges and was named *Outstanding Program of the Year* by 4CSD, a statewide trade association.

3 In the California Community College system, the nation's largest community college system, boards of trustees are publicly elected officials.

4 Dr. Maloney succeeded a superintendent/president who had served as CEO for 20 years.

Green, N. (2015, March 12). ECC president Thomas Fallo to step down in 2016 after 20 years at the helm. *The Daily Breeze.* https://www. dailybreeze.com/2015/03/12/el-camino-college-president-thomas-fallo-to-step-down-in-2016-after-20-years-at-the-helm.

5 See:

Harvey, T. R. (1995). *Checklist to change.* Lanham, MD: ScarecrowEducation.

4

"I Had to Become More Proximal"

Interview with Dr. Katrice Albert

Vice President, Office of Institutional Diversity, University of Kentucky

A portion of this chapter originally appeared in *Women in Higher Education* in October 2014.

Dr. Katrice Albert has served as Vice President, Office of Institutional Diversity at the University of Kentucky since September 2021. Dr. Albert has held similar executive roles at Louisiana State University, the University of Minnesota, the NCAA, and in the private sector, and she is the co-author of several books. I became acquainted with Dr. Albert through our mutual involvement in the National Conference for Race & Ethnicity in Higher Education (NCORE).

Describe your job in one sentence.

My role is to lead efforts across five campuses to reach the University of Minnesota's (U of M) most ambitious equity and diversity goals: increasing structural diversity in recruiting ethnic minority and first generation students and ethnic minority faculty and women in under-represented fields, a campus climate that is both free of bias and nurturing of U of M family members, internal and external partnerships and a focus on alumni to return to U of M as a place to give of their time, talent, and treasures.

What did you major in?

My undergrad is in psychology, master's in community agency counseling, and PhD in counseling psychology.

What would you recommend to readers interested in your field?

Coming from any discipline such as law, counseling, or higher education, one needs to think of diversity as competency-building and aligning one's discipline with diversity work after obtaining a degree. Acquiring competency certificates such as the diversity management certificate offered by Cornell University helps cement diversity work in higher education. The National Association of Diversity Officers in Higher Education's (NADOHE) Fellows Program pairs "newbies" with diversity officers with 10 or more years' experience to offer help and challenge to those new in the game.

What are the most common mistakes you see women in higher education make?

Women come from an ethos of "care for others" and are generally not focused on themselves. The goal of higher education is for the good of other people. Growing the next generation of intellectuals needs to be balanced with caring for yourself. Women tend to be super focused on hard work; they often wait to be guided rather than setting goals for themselves.

Women need to chart their own courses, seek the advice of mentors, and commit to themselves and growing their expertise through programs such as the Bryn Mawr HERS Summer Institute for Women in Higher Education. Women leaders need to decide where they want to be in five years and then in 10 years. When you write this down, you hold yourself accountable.

What was the path to your current position?

Persistence, drive, and passion to become a national thought leader and pacesetter related to diversity.

As a young girl, the women in my community took an interest in me and were positive role models and teachers. As a McNair Scholar, mentors taught me to be thoughtful about graduate studies as a steppingstone to a doctoral degree. I wanted to be a black psychologist, not a psychologist who's black.

When I came to the office of multicultural affairs at Louisiana State University in 2001 as a young leader, Dr. Carolyn Hargraves and Dr. Bonnie Alfred saw me as "a bull in a china shop" and helped finesse my intellect. I was promoted to three positions in 12 years and became the permanent vice president of equity and diversity after serving as interim.

At LSU, I pursued bold strategies to increase structural diversity, which resulted in the highest number of African American and Latino students to join the undergraduate student population, two freestanding cultural centers, and the formation of a National Diversity Advisory Board thoughtful about fundraising to encourage more students of underserved populations to attend graduate school and pursue doctoral studies.

What was the best advice you received along the way?

"To thine own self be true." As a person of color and a young person in higher education administration, being guided in "how to be" was a saving grace for me. In your personal and professional life, live authentically with no regret. Instead of mimicking men, practice your own leadership style with your feet firmly on the ground so that you can sleep at night.

Higher education is a very political animal; you must become a political player in higher education. Finesse your emotional intelligence to navigate political hot water. Use your woman's instinct and be transparent with people you trust, like mentors, to talk through situations. Women need to become effective communicators, verbally and in writing.

What do you value as a leader and diversity officer?

I'm a principle-based, servant leader. As Dr. Martin Luther King Jr. said, "It's always the right time to do the right thing." No job is ever too small or too big. I engage in the day-to-day grind of diversity work and look 5–10 years down the line.

People want to be with winners. Bring people along. Be willing to roll up your sleeves. Let people know you're working alongside them and just as hard to get a vision achieved. I strive to be a visionary leader and see diversity as part of the university's fabric.

What are some goals you have for this year?

Telling the story and innovation of the University of Minnesota's office of diversity, one of the top five offices in the country in terms of staff, budget, and number of offices. We're a model to mimic!

This year, we'll be focused on men of color and the tenets of the My Brother's Keeper initiative. We have a large East African and Hmong population and are working to change the undergraduate experience for them. We're also looking toward a U of M National Advisory Board to develop philanthropic giving in the Twin Cities—home to the most Fortune 500 companies in the country—wherein we align the university's strategic vision with these companies' need for a diverse workforce.

Author's Note: An updated interview with Dr. Albert took place in August 2022.

You have served in executive diversity, equity and inclusion roles at several major universities, the NCAA, and as a private sector consultant. What has been similar and different about these diversity roles, and what have you learned about yourself, DEIA work, and those you serve?

In all the senior roles I have been granted, the leaders with whom I have worked, supported, and served have very good intentions around diversity, equity, inclusion, justice, accessibility, and improved inclusive excellence. However, there was a varied path on how we got there. There's no straight line to claiming victory on these important goals and objectives. We are working together among all sorts of constituencies and expectations and those who donate to our efforts. Many of those whom I have worked for and currently work for have state connections, so we are acquiring resources from state legislatures.

All the leaders have been "best-intentioned" which is very much appreciated. They want to race ahead with the notion of inclusive excellence. They want to go much faster than we have gone before in making sure accessibility and opportunity are there for all, but especially those that are under resourced, underserved, and minoritized. It is also a fact that I have worked for all white men who appreciate diversity, and I must, at times, be their moral compass and most times challenge them in ways that they allowed me to push back gently. The roles have been different in terms of the rate and pace in which I have been able to realize change and have success. I heard it once said sometimes, "you have to slow down to speed up". Additionally, there's an African proverb by which I live my life: "If you want to go fast, go alone, if you want to go far, go together." Neither are easy, but both are true.

What I've learned about myself is that I'm a dreamer, collaborator, and negotiator; I am a problem solver; I am a steward of this work and I want to produce "roots and wings." I want to pour into and grow young scholars so that they can fly. This takes a lot of time, patience, and energy, even when you are struggling with all the "mess and minutia" of higher education. A well-known minister coached me in helping me realize that I must work through all the "mess and minutia", the "m&ms," to get the people who will fly and soar ahead of me to reach their fullest potential. The "m&ms" can often be frustrating and delay and derail the real work, but working through, around, under, and over the "m&ms" gets us to the reason we committed to this purpose-driven work.

I have learned how to be a person who can have brave conversations and offer tough information to leaders who might not want to hear what I have to say nor recommend. I let them know that if we are to get to our ultimate goal of access and opportunity to advance this state institution or this organization, as may be the case, "you must participate in more active listening." I've also learned how to stand back and let other people carry the message. The collaboration effort may be, "let me get with my colleagues—other vice presidents—and let them carry my message in their next 1:1 with our president". Sometimes women leaders must have men carry their message to other men who are in the powerful position. It seems foolish, doesn't it? But it is a strategy that manages the Glass Cliff[1]. Senior women leaders are often hired to do very hard jobs and then we are not supported in the same ways that our men colleagues are supported. Then we must negotiate and play a chess game in nuanced ways.

Women of color, Black women in particular, are given jobs where they cannot have success because we're not given the support that our colleagues are given. We are placed on the Glass Cliff and made to think we can do these hard jobs. We will do our level best to have success and produce with excellence, but we are teetering on a Glass Cliff because we don't have the budgetary resources, we don't have the human capital, we don't have the influential support, like our male colleagues are given; but we are certainly expected to create excellence, innovation, and often expected to achieve unrealistic goals. And we persist toward excellence where racial battle fatigue is realized.

I co-edited a book on racial battle fatigue.[2] Racial battle fatigue comes when people, particularly Black people, are given highly unrealistic goals with limited or no support.

The glass cliff, for me, is defined as follows: I am one of the only senior leaders who happens to be a woman, who happens to be a young, African American woman, who has 25 years in the game and knows the work—in my fourth iteration—without equity in resources. I don't have the support that my white, male colleagues in the vice-presidential role have. Thus, I need them to "carry some of my water" simply because they have greater resources (i.e., budget, people, time, influence, etc.) in every sense of the word.

The Glass Cliff is my new thinking especially as young, Black women executives whom I mentor, coach, advocate, and sponsor are discussing similar experiences I have experienced. I see myself reflected in their challenges. I too have been put on this glass cliff as I work to gain greater resources, more staff, and additional time and influence. Just like my mentees, I'm given all these goals to accomplish by yesterday, so I often wake up at 1:00am with anxiety saying to myself, "I'm behind." And I don't ever run behind because the stereotype that Black people are always late is something I don't want to reinforce. I'm up at 1:00am working my vampire hours. Colleagues say I look so much better these days, and that I look like I'm sleeping better. And I say, "Good, it must be the good foundation and under eye concealer I have from Bobbi Brown Cosmetics."

Gender equity is something which I continue to consider and understand. The Black men on the team don't experience what I'm experiencing. I've got to lean into and understand the gender dynamics. All the men and especially the three Black men who are on the president's cabinet are not having the same experiences I am having. They are very well-endowed. They have the support, and they have the access.

How did the murders of Breonna Taylor, George Floyd, Ahmaud Arbery, and the racial uprising of the summer of 2020 impact your personal experience and career decisions as a DEIA executive who is Black?

The series of murders in 2020 that got attention, because we've had many, many murders even before Emmett Till and the horrors of lynching; but now there are cell phones. Cell phone videos document exactly what happens. The impact of the 2020 murders reinforced my career trajectory to double down and be more like my muse, St. Katharine Drexel,[3] the patron saint of social justice, and the founder of my alma mater, Xavier University of Louisiana. This moment in time reinforced that I am doing the right work in my life. That my life has passion, purpose, and meaning. The murders were hard to watch. To this day, I still have not seen the 10-minute video of the murder of George Floyd, I simply refuse to watch it. The meaning of my life is reinforced by St. Katharine Drexel, who did this work way, way ahead of me. To say that I am working in the legacy and light of this patron saint luminary and continuing her light gave me the privilege to say that I am a national thought leader in the work.

Like most women and people of color, I struggle with imposter syndrome despite having all the education, written books, and given public keynotes on major public stages. People want to hear from me because of this trauma that has happened in our nation and is being viewed internationally. It gave me permission to go after every sector other than higher education, but to use higher education and sport as my foundation. I was able to work with executives in banking, healthcare, and leaders in K-12 education, non-profits, and religious organizations simply because they saw me as a national, higher education thought leader having been in higher ed and sport.

This profession gives me a privilege to say this work is necessary, needed, and vital. If you're a leader and you're not on your culturally competent journey, then you are foregoing a leadership superpower. I will tell and back-light every CEO who would like for me to come into their lives to share: If they are not culturally competent and resist me helping them understand microaggressions, cultural competency, and cultural humility, they are doing themselves and those around them a great disservice. I tell them, "The reason you're calling me is because you're struggling to talk about George Floyd, Breonna Taylor, and Ahmaud Arbery." Until leaders understand their responsibility to grow their cultural intelligence (CQ), EQ, and cultural humility as leadership competencies, they're simply being irresponsible.

The 2020 murders encouraged me back to the traditional role in higher education in Kentucky because I would like this to look like a post-Breonna Taylor, Kentucky, USA. I want the University of Kentucky to be the guiding light for the ways in which we handle social justice, DEIA, inclusive excellence, and forward thinking around access and opportunity for all sorts of people, and all sorts of ways in this state. Breonna Taylor, this young woman, had been a student at the UK, where I currently serve. She stopped out of her degree program to get EMT training, she was doing EMT work, and then got shot in her sleep. You can imagine my heartbreak that Breonna Taylor has a history with our university because she started as an undergraduate student, stepped out to make money to pay for her undergraduate work, got the EMT certification, worked on being able to support people under stress and in crisis as an EMT specialist, and then got shot in her sleep.

I would not have come back to a traditional role after two years as an executive consultant. As a consultant, you're not pushing a boulder up a mountain as you do in a traditional, academic DEIA role. Dr. Eli Capilouto, President of the University of Kentucky, inspired me to advance Kentucky in a post-Breonna Taylor, Kentucky, USA. How could

I advance this state with him in honor of this young woman? Having been a former student who stepped out to get this training in emergency medical technician work, did the work, and then got killed in her sleep—goodness, my people can't even sleep! I am doing the responsible thing, in the light of St. Katharine Drexel, by coming to the University of Kentucky. I selected this position to honor this young woman and because, in her honor, other people need to have access to and opportunities in higher education.

What do you consider to be the most significant challenge and the greatest accomplishment you've realized during your career trajectory?

The good work does not come easily. I have heard it once said, "women hold up half the sky." What I know to be true is that women in higher education certainly hold up at least half the sky, if not more. The greatest challenges have come in around convincing those who don't see inclusive excellence as a part of higher education's thrust for changing lives as a real thing. When we lean into inclusive excellence and DEI work, the support of those who are underserved and under resourced, we are changing the trajectory of entire families, right? It is challenging. However, I've learned over the course of my career how to help show people that DEI work can be and shall be win-win. It's more about the strategy and showing how we can reduce costs by sharing resources to do great university work than by simply trying to change hearts.

At first, I got into the work around a moral compass, an ethos of care, an ethic of love. I've gotten better over time. Realizing that I needed to make better relationships with people who might not have agreed with anything that I thought. Those who are more traditionalists in higher education—(read conservative colleagues)—must become some of my very best friends, colleagues, advocates, and sponsors. Imagine how challenging this is because I must have very difficult and critical conversations and lean into things I don't want to hear and try to figure out how to make compromise.

During my career trajectory at Louisiana State University (LSU), where I was hired and then promoted three times in 12 years, I became the best of friends/colleagues with the CFO. Early on, I didn't realize the need because I was young and naïve in this career. Then I realized if I were to get more resources for students who were under-served and under resourced, then I would need to go to the person with the purse or the old school way of saying it, the pocketbook! He and I couldn't be more different. I had to have the CFO understand that there were faces behind every move that he made in allocating resources from the state. At every one of the career stops, I made the best of friends and asked to be mentored by the CFO. It was almost like a life hack i.e. if I were going to do well in the role, the CFO had to mentor me. I had to hear their challenges, and they had to hear mine. I wasn't going to be divorced from them because I was angry that I didn't get the allocation that other people received. *I had to become more proximal.* In the chal-lenges, I learned unique ways of being.

I just had a session with my team on emotional intelligence and how EQ outweighs IQ in every metric in terms of the resources you acquire and the promotions that you get. If you're relational and you're smart enough, you must also have the political savvy and relationships to get to where you need to be. The challenges have come with learning. We don't fail, we just have new learnings.

The greatest accomplishments have been the number of students that I supported to the terminal degree (i.e., doctoral, medical, dental, and law degrees). There are lot of superlatives in my career background, but it's nothing like seeing your students get to the terminal degree in their fields, and that they will be your legacy. I know that I stand on broad shoulders. My greatest accomplishment in higher education has been fostering someone from their very first day of college, where they may have been a first generation, under resourced student, to seeing them get the terminal degree and helping them all along. It's very powerful to stick with someone, and someone stuck with me until this point, and I know I wasn't easy and I'm still not. I can talk about national awards I've received or buildings that I've helped to realize, but these things pale in comparison to witnessing students reaching their greatest potential. For me, it's witnessing them reach that terminal degree, getting people to the finish line.

I tell anyone who will listen that I want to be graduated to be the Valerie Jarett of higher education. In her own right, she is a remarkable woman, but she was in the background mentoring, cajoling, and massag-ing the Obamas to get to the White House. Of all the things I've done in my career, I'm best at being in the background getting folks to race ahead of me. That's when you reduce the ego and see that there are so many people better than I am out here.

Significant data distinguishes differences between men and women leaders regarding negotiating and asking for what they want in the workplace.[4] How have you navigated and/or grown in this area during your career?

I was not good at negotiating in the beginning, at all. People will say that I was better than I thought I was at first, so when I talk about the negotiation tactics that I used in the beginning, people say, "Wow, I should have used that!", "I have certainly gotten better" over time just knowing my worth and learning from those who had done very strategic moves in order to elevate salary, title, and get more resources for their units. Sitting at the knees of others to ask, "How did you get this? Why do you have this beautiful office that is well-appointed and we're in the dungeon?" It has been coaching and mentoring, it has been practicing and sometimes failing, and being a Southern woman who wants to be courted. I have used some of these same techniques getting to the top spot in terms of the candidate pool and then letting the offer sit: "Let me think about this job."

If organizations can't manage what I'm expecting, then I say, "It might be best to go to your next candidate; that might be the right person for the role." I've also said no to roles that were really intriguing simply because they would not pay me what I know my colleagues made. Equity in salary for me is a real thing, and I was dealing with leaders who had never been told "no". By saying "no", suddenly, I got more intriguing. It's been an art and a science of reading negotiation books for women, asking people to coach me on how to negotiate, figuring out how other people got what they wanted, and a bit of mystique in being a Southern woman saying, "Oh no, Southern women appreciate the chase." Both my parents taught me about "old school courting"; they did not allow me to just go on dates. They expected my dates to come in, greet them, and sit on the couch across from me while they supervised from the room next door.

Negotiation is like a waltz. To be able to really want a new role because it's the next great thing in my career and then to say, "You know, respectfully, I must decline for all these reasons, the salary just doesn't justify the move. I have my grandparents and my parents here in Louisiana, so why would I come to your institution for this amount of money (much less than colleagues) and lose out on the richness of my family?" Or I would say, "I respectfully decline. Maybe your next candidate is better than me." It's been an art and a science.

I highly suggest to all women leaders that as they traverse the country and each time they are moving, that they are moving with an elevated experience and they're getting exactly what they want because they've been coached, they've watched negotiations, they've read the books, they've looked at TedTalks, practiced with their spouse, significant other, or friends about how to go into a meeting where they need to discuss compensation packages, and they need to do it well. It's always joy.

When you were interviewed in 2014, you referenced a 10-year plan developed through the H.E.R.S. Leadership Institute.[5] To what extent did you stick to your original plan? What changes or modified decisions took place along the way?

That life planning exercise was just remarkable, and I thought I had the world by storm. It was the last thing I did during the H.E.R.S. process. Once I did the plan, I saw this was my life and I've used the plan as an example when I talk to students, peers, or other mentees about how to think through creating a career map. I've stuck to this plan for the most part because I always reflect when I look at it and realize, "Wow, I've done so many things."

At this point in my career, I'm doing what I want, right? I've had every one of the roles described in that 10-year plan from then until now. I can affirm that I am in the place in my career that I have chosen. I want every woman to get to a place where they say to themselves, "I want this job because I chose this job, and this job chose me. I'm in it because I want it." Coming to be a VP of diversity in a traditional role while consulting is to be in Kentucky, a post-Breonna Taylor, Kentucky, USA, to work with Dr. Eli Capiloutto. I'm doing exactly what I want, and I would love that for women who are younger than I am. I want this goal to be reached for women so much earlier in their careers, in their late 30s or early 40s, as I make the half-century mark this year. Getting all the education that they need, the experience, and then saying, "I'm ready to take on the world, and I'm going to take a job that I want!"

What Can We Learn?

Dr. Albert inspires women leaders to value their worth and care for themselves while growing the next generation of intellectuals in higher education. She emphasizes the importance of women living authentically with no regret and practicing their leadership style rather than mimicking that of men. She asserts higher education is a political animal; therefore, women must finesse their emotional intelligence to navigate political waters. Dr. Albert emphasizes a willingness to roll up one's sleeves and work alongside others to achieve a shared vision. She strives to be a visionary leader and diversity to be part of the university's fabric. Dr. Albert cautions that women and women of color, in particular, are placed in positions where they strive for success and excellence but are not provided the same resources to achieve as their male colleagues, a phenomenon known as the glass cliff effect.

Notes

1 The Glass Cliff Effect refers to a phenomenon where women and underrepresented minoritized groups break through a glass ceiling in obtaining senior leadership positions only to find themselves in precarious, under-resourced roles. See:

Morgenroth, T., Kirby, T. A., Ryan, M. K., & Sudkämper, A. (2020). The who, when, and why of the glass cliff phenomenon: A meta-analysis of appointments to precarious leadership positions. *Psychological Bulletin, 146*(9), 797–829. https://doi.org/10.1037/bul0000234.

Evidence suggests that women are more likely to be selected for roles in times of crisis, an effect amplified in countries with higher gender inequality.

When a woman leader is chosen during a time of crisis, downturn, or conflict in an organization, this type of high-risk leadership assignment may also be aligned with women leaders taking the blame if the organization does not rapidly improve under their leadership and may then suffer falling off the glass cliff. See:

Murrell, A. (2018, December 3). The new wave of women leaders: Breaking the glass ceiling or facing the glass cliff?" *Forbes* 12/3/2018, https://www.paisboa.org/assets/aggie-blog/2019/05.03.19/The%20 New%20Wave%20Of%20Women%20Leaders_%20Breaking%20The%20 Glass%20Ceiling%20Or%20Facing%20The%20Glass%20Cliff_.pdf.

Among women profiled in this book, some pointed to feeling the need to work constantly at the expense of getting sufficient sleep and attending to self-care. They suggested male counterparts may be better positioned in terms of human capital and other resources, a seemingly double-edged sword.

2 Fasching-Varner, K.J., Albert, K.A., Mitchell, R., & Allen, C.A. (Eds.). (2014). *Racial battle fatigue in higher education: Exposing the myth of post-racial America.* New York: Rowman & Littlefield.

3 St. Katharine Drexel, born in 1858 into wealth in Philadelphia, ministered to African Americans and American Indians based on the example of her parents becoming an apostle to the oppressed, founded the Sister of the Blessed Sacrament, founded more than 250 schools including Xavier University in 1925, and later became a saint. See:

The life and legacy of our foundress: Saint Katharine Drexel (2020, March 3). Xavier University Archives. https://www.xula.edu/news/2020/03/the-life-and-legacy-of-our-foundress-saint-katharine-drexel.html.

4 See:

Babcock, L., & Laschever, S. (2003). Women don't ask: Negotiation and the gender divide. Princeton, NJ: Princeton University Press.

5 See Appendix for suggested professional development programs.

5

"The Best Way to Move Forward is to be Absolutely Great at Your Job"

Interview with Dr. Jane Close Conoley

President, California State University, Long Beach

A portion of this chapter originally appeared in *Women in Higher Education* in January 2016.

Dr. Jane Close Conoley is the first woman to be appointed President of California State University, Long Beach where she began her tenure in July 2014. A psychologist by training, Dr. Conoley is a prolific writer, and the author, co-author, or editor of more than 120 books, articles, and book chapters. I became acquainted with Dr. Conoley through my doctoral program in educational leadership at CSU Long Beach.

Describe your job in one sentence.

I see my job as president as creating environments that facilitate the success of the community. I'm a psychologist, so I understand the difficulties of personal change. My own personal theory of psychology evolved to a more ecological understanding.

Women in the Higher Education C-Suite: Diverse Executive Profiles, First Edition.
Lisa Mednick Takami.
© 2024 John Wiley & Sons, Inc. Published 2024 by John Wiley & Sons, Inc.

I see my job as increasing support for faculty, students and staff, decreasing the number of hassles, keeping us in touch with a larger environment so we don't miss important future or current forces that could undermine our viability.

It really is a systems approach. My job is to make sure that we are an example of a healthy system. We support people, we give them feedback, but we're open to environmental influences and we're agile and responsive enough to avoid difficulties and take advantage of opportunities. That's not easy in a bureaucratic system like ours, so there's a lot of work to be done.

How were your educational experiences formative in envisioning the role of a college presidency?

Very early, before I had a career, my entire K–16 education was in women's schools. In that early experience, all the leadership roles were open to me. All the influential, powerful people were women. I have to believe that these experiences had an important influence.

I remember coming to the University of Texas at Austin, [where she received her PhD in school psychology] walking into the first class I ever had with men and thinking, "I wonder if I'm as smart as I think I am", and confirming I *was* as smart as I had believed.

I had never compared myself before. That early developmental mentoring was really important. I certainly have a level of confidence that comes from having been able to be president of my student council. I went to school at a time when it would have been much more likely for the boy to have been president and the girl vice president. There were no boys—we always had to problem-solve for ourselves.

You are a prolific writer. What impact does your writing have on your job as president?

A big part of a president's job is communication. My focus on writing as a professor and as a researcher has really helped me communicate more clearly. Writing has helped me to be a better speaker, organize a sentence, and get it out.

The good news is that the background of writing textbooks and articles has given me a store of information and the ability to go look for information that is really helpful as I make decisions and communicate

to people why we should go in a particular direction, what the latest research is [on a topic], and if the research is applicable to our context.

Which individuals or mentors have had the greatest impact on your professional development?

There are a few people that really stand out. When I was at the University of Nebraska-Lincoln, they hired a provost, Joan Leitzel, and Joan was the first to be hired at that most senior academic level.

I remember being with a group interviewing her and how she answered each interview question by citing a very specific source. She didn't use vast, glossy generalizations. She took the questions very seriously and specifically, which was in stark contrast to other experiences I'd had and informed me that if I have nothing to say, say nothing, and if I have something to say, provide some evidence.

Eventually, I was associate dean at the University of Nebraska, and the dean, Jim O'Hanlon, was a tremendous model of positive leadership. He always looked for people's intentions. He didn't get caught up in aggressive, obnoxious personalities, but focused on what people were trying to do.

O'Hanlon encouraged partnering with people in their intentions and dreams rather than getting put off by their awkward attempts to make something happen. Sometimes, people in a group are acting so sarcastic or demeaning, and I think to myself, "What this person is trying to do is make sure that I understand the importance of, for example, faculty salaries. So, let me ignore the method and try to connect with the person on the outcome or the result."

Another important person was Robert Gates, who was president of Texas A&M for a number of years while I was dean there. He was a person of great integrity but also amazingly smart politically.

Given the very conservative context of Texas A&M, Gates managed to accomplish some really important things. For a long time, Texas universities couldn't use race as an admissions variable, and then the court reversed itself. Instead, Robert Gates raised $8 million to fund learning communities and scholarships for first-generation students.

This idea was brilliant because most Texas Aggies who were giving money at the time were first-generation. He raised the enrollment of underrepresented groups by 35% that first year, as I recall. True, the numbers were small to begin with, but he attached learning communities and had high success with these students who otherwise would not have been able to afford to attend.

What would you recommend to readers interested in pursuing a college presidency?

There are many opportunities to get leadership experiences like the ACE Fellows program or the Harvard Leadership program. Many of the vice presidents and presidents I meet have gone through these programs, so obviously there's a real benefit.

You can come to the presidency from a variety of pathways and backgrounds—student affairs, chief financial officer, or someone more out of the box like Janet Napolitano [former president of the University of California system and former Secretary of Homeland Security].

There are opportunities, but you have to put yourself out there to be the department chair or dean (on the academic side), and the best way to move forward is to be absolutely great at what you do.

Academia is changing. The funding models are changing very dramatically in public higher education. There'll probably be more and more openings for a nontraditional path—a businesswoman, a politician, the head of a foundation like the Lumina Foundation.

I'm guessing [this will be the case] because there's so much ebb and flow in how we have to think about keeping public higher education as a viable element to our society.

What do you consider to be your greatest successes?

I've maintained positive working relationships with many, many groups. Most people would say that the department or college worked better when I was there. People got along better.

I didn't take sides. I was clear. I told the truth as I knew it. I sometimes was wrong, but I told it as I knew it. Looking back on a long career, I consider it a success that I haven't left a long trail of broken relationships, as many others have told me they have.

What would you like to be your imprint at CSULB?

At CSU Long Beach, it's a little early in my tenure, but by the time I leave the university, I look forward to our being much more densely and richly partnered with community agencies, whether they be hospitals, K–12, community colleges or businesses. In my mind, that's the future of the university.

I would also hope that people say of The Beach, "This is the best place to work" and students would say, "What a good choice it was to come here."

Author's Note: An updated interview took place with Dr.Conoley in February 2022 reflecting her leadership development and campus circumstances since the start of the Covid-19 pandemic.

How did the murders of George Floyd, Breonna Taylor, and Ahmaud Arbery and the racial reckoning of 2020 impact you as a leader? How did the institution respond?

Following those murders, there was such a huge awareness about the targeting of Black Americans by police that it was the right time to redouble our antiracist practices. I spent about three days (cumulatively with 15 different groups) listening to how CSULB was experienced by Black campus members and community members. Those conversations turned into an equity plan which is still guiding our DEI efforts today. The *Equity and Action Report* is on our website with updates.[1]

Across the campus many other Divisions, Departments, Colleges and programs developed their own plans. We changed the name of the President's Commission on Inclusive Excellence to the President's Equity and Change Commission. We were accepted by AAC&U to be a Center for Truth, Racial Healing, and Transformation; we have or soon will have hired DEI directors in four of five of our Divisions (Academic Affairs, Student Affairs, Administration and Finance and University Relations and Development). We devoted all last year's convocation elements to DEI presentations and have required all staff to be trained in implicit bias. Many faculty have also elected to take part in various DEI workshops.

We've set up regular meetings with various affinity groups (Black, Latinx, Asian) and have fast tracked the construction of cultural affinity group spaces. We've also re-vamped some of our outreach efforts to prospective Black students and added advocacy advocates to all faculty search committees.

You have led CSU Long Beach through the unprecedented time of the COVID-19 pandemic. What has been most challenging during this time? What has been most rewarding? How will the pandemic shift university operations moving forward?

The pandemic certainly presented the leadership team and me with a new level of threat. Many times, we face "reputational threat" or the need to handle a situation well and communicate. For the first time in my career, we were facing a threat that would kill people. We had one staff member, sadly, who died, and at least one other who is still dealing with heart issues associated with getting Covid. There have been sad and scary moments around losing a staff member.

We did not have a playbook, and that was very challenging. In consultation with the CSU system, we determined that we had to move to alternative instruction, but at first, we thought it would be for a few weeks or a month. The constantly changing timeline created so much ambiguity, which we were not used to. At some level, a leadership position is filled with ambiguity, and you never have enough data to be sure of your decisions, but in this case, there were so many factors out of our control in terms of public health. We could make plans, but the virus was in charge. At first, I was following the former playbook that we communicate when we have an answer, but early on, I realized people needed more communication, even if the communication was that we did not know when we would return to in-person instruction, etc.

At the beginning, I started a video series sitting at my dining room table. At first, it was a sort of palliative measure showing what the police were doing, what the cleaning people were doing, etc. Despite health concerns, the communications team insisted we hire a professional videographer, but the goal was that I wanted to give people a sense of how the teams were pulling together. Then, from listening to faculty, I got the sense that people were desperate for information, so we switched to an approach of "here's what we know now" and we planned whom we might interview next such as the head of student health services. I received good feedback to these interviews and have continued them.

On the positive side, it was a pleasure to be involved with my team and see that they could jump into constant problem-solving. We discovered there were no simple problems. Any decision had layers of impact on staff. In team meetings, I started asking, "Does anyone have a simple problem? Let's do that one first!" The idea was to start with a slam-dunk problem and feel good, but there were no slam dunks. One change was that we had to get into tighter relationships with the city's public health department and new vendors to help us with testing and vaccine protocols. We forged more relationships with the city of Long Beach and various city entities than we had before, and that is a good thing. We want to make sure we keep these relationships, strive to be good partners, and not back away from our partners' advice. We developed new protocols for cleaning and upgrading our air filtration system as we learned more about how the virus is transmitted; those changes will be longstanding improvements to maintain a safe environment.

In the future, I am sure we will have more online and hybrid courses. Many faculty enjoyed teaching online. Before the pandemic, only 4% of our courses or programs were fully online with a few more hybrid courses. Suddenly, that figure jumped to 96%. I was impressed with the flexibility of everyone to make that degree of change even if it may have been begrudgingly. Now, the online classes of multi-section courses are filling first. Everyone returning to campus is joyful about the return, but people have discovered that it is more fun not to have to look for a parking space, particularly on our campus.

The effect on staff will be longstanding. We have learned that we can do some jobs remotely and do not need everyone on campus from 8–5 to do a good job. We have developed a pattern of more flexible student services like advising and telehealth; much will stick because it made us a more accessible campus. We will be using some of our remote capacity to enlarge the number of service hours we offer. It is hard to bring a full workforce in from 5:00–9:00 pm, but it is easier to accomplish this when dividing those who are working from home and those who are in the office.

One problem has certainly been freshmen and sophomores who began their freshman year or were finishing their senior year of high school during the pandemic. We have seen a drop in their credit load and a drop in persistence rates particularly among our students of color. When we have taken a deep dive look at our data, persistence rates among non-URM (non-underrepresented minority) students have stayed the same or increased slightly; rates for our URM (underrepresented minority) students have decreased. I have heard this trend expressed from presidents of nearby urban universities indicating a disproportionate impact on students of color. This is an issue we need to worry about; we are problem-solving, putting some services on steroids, and trying to get more student affairs services and academic strategies in place to support these students' success.

How do you lead through unexpected changes in your leadership team, and what would you recommend to leaders forced to embrace constant change?

At one level, the only constant *is* change. We have had so many people decide to retire or look for something else that we are having some staffing challenges. One way to manage during unexpected changes is to have relationships with people so they come and tell you about expected changes ahead of time. With our Provost, who retired last year, he and I had spoken more than once about his growing conviction to retire. I must admit that I thought I had convinced him to stay, but after Christmas that year, he had decided it was time. We also lost our Vice President of University Relations and Development, but she had also given me a heads up, and I had been working on a salary package, but working in a public system, it is hard to move quickly on something like that because I could not ask the Chancellor for more money for a vice president until after the CFA contract for faculty had been negotiated; the optics would have been terrible.

In the ways you manage your team, you strive to have the relationships that allow these important conversations to happen i.e. nobody is working behind your back. Also, I always try to surround myself with people who can talk to me about a change, and I remain open to changing my mind. During the pandemic, I was very concerned that we had closed our childcare center because I knew faculty, students, and staff who were parents could not operate at optimal levels without childcare. We had a decision to make about whether we would re-open the childcare center by following Covid protocols for that point in time. I remember arriving at that meeting absolutely convinced that we had to re-open, that reopening would be hard and expensive, but that we had to do it. During the conversation, however, I rethought my position and decided I needed to follow the lead of those who had expertise, who knew how to run a childcare center, and who understood the potential threats.

Part of my approach is the willingness to listen to other people and take expertise; that helps me. Also, part of my template of life and one of my slogans with my team is "there is always something" i.e., to understand that this is how life and the universe unfold; we are constantly given surprises. I do not have an emotional reaction when problems present. Instead, I think, "Oh, here it comes," and that helps. I can tell people notice this and say, "It's such a relief you're so unflappable." Whatever gets put on the table, I think, "okay, now this situation is on the table."

I had to remind members of the team that no one gets thrown under the bus here, that we are all in a growth mindset, we all screw up, and I must model that approach to make it real. Depending on the setting that leaders have come from, they must learn this approach as well. Of course, we have to "walk the walk" in managing conflict. For example, at the end of last semester, I could tell that two of the vice presidents had more tension over being short-staffed and were discussing remote and in-person work schedules and an issue one had with HR. Automatically, I said out loud, "Are you two fighting?", and they started to laugh. Some of my approach, having trained and practiced as a therapist, is to follow my instincts about how to identify a conflict and not diffuse things, but make it more normalized for people to talk it out. Equanimity is very important because people cannot follow you if you are always falling apart.

The other thing I try to do is to let people know when I am having challenges in my own life by saying, "I am a little distracted" and perhaps sharing part of what is going on with me. I may add, "Ask me twice if I don't respond, and don't think it's about you because it's really about me" to head off any attributions they may have about my not being interested or available as usual. That helps the team keep on an even level. We have a new provost and an interim vice president for development, so we are needing to do teambuilding all over again; it is a constant process. Something I have learned more dramatically in this role is how purposeful I need to be about building the leadership team. I just wrote the six-month evaluation of the new Provost, and I indicated that it is vital to me that they work to build trusting and close relationships with the other vice presidents and make sure they know I do not see them just operating individually; they must figure out how to work with others.

What have you learned during your eight years in serving as the first woman president of CSU Long Beach?

The whole labor-management relationship was new and so foreign to me because I had not served previously in an environment where faculty were unionized. I was surprised that people would view me as someone other than an academic colleague since so much of my professional life had been in the classroom and writing books. There was a lot of learning there. There was a time when the CFA (California Faculty Association, the faculty union) came outside my window and were chanting, so I followed my instinct to go down and talk with them. I was dressed appropriately, but I do not "dress for success" per se. One of the faculty members said, "It's like you're just one of us." And I said, "I *am* one of you, that's exactly it!"

Recently, I was giving advice to some of the other CSU presidents during the most recent faculty union negotiations after I had said, "I hope you get the best contract you can because when you're happy, I'm happy." I say this every time negotiations come up; it has stuck, and people believe it. I appeared jointly with the CFA co-chair, and I reiterated that obviously I wanted them to get the best deal that they could and that I did not want a strike. At a recent Academic Senate meeting, one CFA member said that anybody who knows me knows this is true and I thought, "Yay!" People have been socialized in the CSU (California State University system) to see issues as "us" and "them" when it comes to so-called "labor-management". I understand this dynamic is part of our existence, but I have nurtured what came before me in fostering almost no labor issues e.g., we have not issued a grievance in more than two years. We have instituted a consultative program where if someone has an issue, they do not have to go into the grievance process. Our HR will consult with both parties to resolve the difference. That was the CFA's idea which I supported and was very positive about when they presented it to me. Ironically, a lot of my early research was on how we go about consulting with people without professionals to help resolve issues, so I thought, "yay", and I did not assign them to read books I had written on the topic.

I have the advantage of having been trained as a psychologist and having been trained extensively, due to my interests and advisors, at the individual and organizational levels. This has made a huge difference. In my best moments, I see a lot of behavior as reflecting an organizational need, not a personal deficit. I fall off that wagon sometimes and I get frustrated, but Tim White (former CSU Chancellor) once said to me that you need to adopt the lens that every conversation is the first conversation so that you are not entering the discussion with animus and negative expectations. Instead, you are entering the conversation like you want to be present and learn from it. It is a high bar, but I do remind myself of this lens when I anticipate that it will be a contentious conversation and that I should not go in with defensive forces up.

The last eight years have taught me to be more decisive as I have grown into the reality that I am "the decider" on so many things. For example, students recently wrote me regarding changes to graduation that they wanted to see. They wrote that "we know you're not the final word on this" and I wrote back to them, "I am the final word on this, everyone else is a messenger." I was trying to make the point that they should not be mean to everyone else, which had been the case. At the same time, more than ever, I am more reliant on team members to inform my final decisions because I am surrounded by fabulous expertise.

Rather than go it alone, I always have that team support. I have learned to let some things go; I have learned not everything deserves my attention. I was hard-wired that if you wrote me an email, I wrote you an email back. Now I know that there are certain people that I should not engage with because they are involved with a grievance in some other way, and my jumping in is just going to confuse the process. I have changed some of my patterns and am much more comfortable. At first, I was very uncomfortable when I would get advice from a lawyer to not engage with a particular individual. That would really bother me because I would think, "they're waiting for a reply, they wrote to me." Now I am much more at home with the need not to respond sometimes.

I am very curious about everything happening on the campus, and I have certainly learned to trust in others. I ended up needing to fire a vice president. When I reflected on that situation, I realized I had had concerns about that person for several years. She was not hired by me, but at the same time I was hired. In the learning process together, I did not listen to all the signals that, upon reflection, I had received. I should have given her a graceful exit two years earlier rather than trying to keep coming up with rationales to keep her on board. Now, when I have a doubt on a personnel issue, I am much more willing to act on that doubt.

A very strong weakness in my early leadership positions was that I saw every personnel issue as "this person needs coaching". I was not taking advantage of the fact that if, after six months, this person who was showing me the best that they could do during probation did not belong at the institution. It was never about content, always about relationships. It is not my job to develop every single member of the team. At the time, I was teaching therapy and thought that "this person needs some help." I cannot always be the helper.

Looking back at your career trajectory, what are you most proud of, and is there anything you wish you had done differently?

On the administrative side, I am proud of things I accomplished organizationally whether it was increasing grant dollars or reducing conflict or adding prestige. I am equally and perhaps even more proud that I had a period of my career when I was a serious scholar and viewed as a serious scholar. I know that background has helped me obtain these administrative posts in higher ed; there is a bit of a paradox there. Just because you can write a book does not mean you know how to run an organization. I am very proud of my scholarship which gave me time to think deeply about various areas of study that have proved to be very helpful such as organizational effectiveness and process.

Both my husband and I did a lot of post-doctoral study in family therapy; very soon in my career as a department chair, I thought of my life as doing family therapy. I see situations through this lens, whether they are communication breakdowns, in-group or out-group relations, being too rigid versus letting outside information in, etc. I have had to accept that I cannot please everyone; that is a little painful because I would like to please everyone. My skin is a little thicker, but more importantly, leaders must figure out what their guiding values are.

I listened very deeply recently to these students who wanted their names read out loud when walking across the stage at graduation. It is a very strong value of mine to promote success, but then I had to realize what the toll would be on the staff during a staffing crisis in considering how many people could we bring to a stadium and how long would they have to stay, 7:00 am-9:00 pm? Burnout is apparent in many staff because we have people leaving. Finding a values-based anchor helps me become more comfortable with difficult decisions. This has been true all along, even in firing the vice president that I alluded to before: I must have people tell me the truth all the time. If I do not believe this is the case, it is not useful because a lot of my information comes through heads of the divisions. Once I lose confidence in being told the truth, I cannot move forward with the same person.

Learning the finances of higher ed has been a whole new area of study for me. I was never a provost. I came from being a dean to being a chancellor (at UC Riverside) and a president. I had never managed a budget beyond the college level; at the college level, you get what the university gives you. You do not need to think about the governor's budget.

Our family motto is, "Things always work out." Earlier in my career, I was on the speakers' circuit, I delivered lectures at conferences, and served as a consultant to many organizations. Looking back, I see I wasted a lot of time sitting on airplanes, but all those experiences gave me an understanding of multiple organizations. Once I served as a consultant to the Army, and it was so instructive. I asked them about goals, and they said, "There is only one goal—mission success." I thought, "that really clarifies things, doesn't it?"

Having those experiences with mental health agencies, many educational agencies, etc. gave me a level of comfort and confidence in dealing with complexity; I had the chance to learn from a lot of people. At the micro level, I would have done some things differently, but at the macro level, it all turned out for the best. For example, if I had not been the interim chancellor at UC Riverside, at the request of the then-president of the UC system, Mark Yudoff, I certainly would not be sitting in this chair as president of CSU Long Beach. Exposure from Tim White, who became Chancellor of the CSU system and whom I had not known previously, liked what I did when I was in his former role at UC Riverside; he pursued me for this job through the search firm. I like the expression, "When one door closes, another door opens."

For whatever reason, I have had many doors open to me, and I have consistently walked through them to see what was on the other side. It has not always been pleasant, but I learned a lot. If I had known I wanted to be a president, I may have made life easier by going to be an ACE (American Council on Education) Fellow, but I was always happy with what I was doing. I have read about research in this area i.e. that people who are most successful are mainly focused on doing a good job with their current job rather than always striving for the next one. I always give this advice e.g., when a student comes in and says they want to be a college president, I always say, "Great! It's a great job, but don't announce that when you're interviewing to be an assistant professor."

What Can We Learn?

Dr. Conoley has always prioritized collegial relationships, and she emphasizes the importance of verbal and written communication. Her background in psychology and the influence of significant mentors taught her to seek stakeholders' meaning whether their words were welcome or rough. She has learned strategic engagement with stakeholders, including the need not to respond to certain emails, and the value of building a trusted team with whom she partners to keep abreast of the university's complex organization. Dr. Conoley acknowledges that earlier in her career, she believed personnel issues amounted to a need for coaching. She came to understand that she cannot always be the helper, and sometimes needs to make difficult personnel decisions for the benefit of the institution.

Note

1 California State University, Long Beach (2020). *Equity and Action Report* https://www.csulb.edu/sites/default/files/2022/documents/dei-report.pdf.

6

"Your Path isn't Necessarily a Straight Line"
Interview with Dr. Sandra Boham

President, Salish Kootenai Community College

Dr. Sandra Boham was named President of Salish Kootenai College in February 2016. Salish Kootenai is a public tribal land-grant community college in Pablo, Montana. Dr. Boham is an enrolled member of the Confederated Salish and Kootenai Tribes of the Flathead Indian Reservation of Montana. I became acquainted with Dr. Boham through writing this book and my interest in elevating the work of Tribal Colleges.

Describe your job in one sentence.

My job is about building relationships to create the best opportunities for the students in our community and for our tribal nation.

Women in the Higher Education C-Suite: Diverse Executive Profiles, First Edition.
Lisa Mednick Takami.
© 2024 John Wiley & Sons, Inc. Published 2024 by John Wiley & Sons, Inc.

What have been the significant steps in your educational and professional journey leading to your present position?

The most significant step was my parents pushing me to go to college. I am a first-generation college graduate and neither of my parents had the opportunity to go to college. When they were pushing me, I wasn't always the most cooperative, but it was probably the best gift they could have given to push me forward. That decision started the whole of my career path and created opportunities and experiences that I wouldn't have had otherwise.

I was always focused on social justice. Going to college and having the experiences I've had allowed me to work on a social justice agenda because that is what tribal colleges are about. I was told early in my career, by one of my mentors, that you need to be flexible, to be mentored, and that sometimes you don't know why your path takes you where it does. You get to places you wouldn't have gone if you hadn't made the choices you made or accepted the opportunities that came your way. Your path isn't necessarily a straight line. It can be really zig zagging and then you get to these incredible places that you wouldn't have landed had your choices been different.

I started doing adult basic education for the college when I was 19. I worked for the Montana Women's Correctional Center implementing their education programs. When they opened their very first Montana site, I never saw myself being in corrections and that was an interesting path, but I learned a lot about barriers and what kinds of choices put people on one path as opposed to another. Then I came back to the college and worked in a Tribal work experience program which transitioned people off public assistance by allowing them to take training and courses. That was an amazing program! Then I became the registrar and director of admissions, so I learned a lot about the processes and accreditation.

Then I left and went to Northern California and worked at CSU Humboldt along with my husband. He is from Great Falls, Montana, but I met him in a graduate program because I was on a fellowship that aimed to increase the enrollment of Tribal College folks. I was in a master's degree program, and he was in a doctoral program. Eventually I followed him to California and worked in the Northern California Indian Development Council (NCIDC), which was very interesting. We served several different small tribes in Northern California in Eureka, Arcada,

and Crescent City. I learned a lot about social service support, job training, and job placement. I was teaching at Humboldt State and College of the Redwoods in their NAS (Native American Studies) department. I would have never thought that the NCIDC position would have put me on this trajectory; it was a totally different type of social services position which I did for 15 years.

When we returned home to Montana, I worked in the college's Upward Bound and GearUp! programs and then transitioned into financial aid and learned all the pre-college outreach and financial aspects of supporting the students. Then my husband got a job in Great Falls with his tribe, the Little Shell Band of Chippewa Indians of Montana, and I became the director of the Indian Education Program for the Great Falls public school district. I had never worked in K-12. My job was to improve outcomes for American Indian students in their school district, so I did a lot of what's called critical race theory now, which was culturally-competent education and leadership. That was a huge turning point for me because I could see how these native students in these off-reservation schools were getting a message that was not good for them. I knew those messages were being transmitted on the reservation, but I didn't know they were also being given in the off-reservation environment. I learned a lot of tools for navigating this scenario as an adult.

I returned to the college as the academic vice president. When the president I was working with passed away after a very short time, I became the president. Strangely enough, all of the teaching, student support services, and social work, all of these experiences came together in this odd mixture that has really helped to inform much of what we see in meeting student support and building programs in our community. Pieces and parts of my career that I never realized would fit into this role as president coalesced.

The person who encouraged me the most to pursue a doctorate was my husband. I had a really rough go of my master's program; it wasn't the academic part. It was institutional racism. There were thirty of us in a Fellows program for American Indians from all of the Tribal Colleges in Montana. The graduate school had never had that many American Indians in a graduate program, ever. The pushback was that the Fellows program was not holding us to the same standards as everyone else. We fought our way through those programs. It made me say to myself, "Not only am I going to get this master's degree, but I'm also going to go on and get my doctorate because someone said I can't." I had to wait until my husband was finished with his doctorate and I had a young child, so I got my doctorate later in life. It was really important because if I was saying, "Education is really important," then I needed to demonstrate that to our community. I did it! Getting my doctorate was also to give back to the community, to be that person who demonstrated it wasn't too late. If I could do it, anyone could do it, right? Completing the doctoral program included some of the best experiences I have had. The research I gave back was important, and I'm always encouraging other people to do the same thing.

How would you describe your leadership approach? How has your leadership style been shaped by being Native American[1] among women who lead Tribal Colleges?

My leadership approach is to try to be collaborative and inclusive. I only know so much. Surround yourself and bring people to the institution who know way more than you do to talk with to create the best possible environment for the students that we serve in our community. The more voices we have, the better decisions we make and the further we can take the college. If you think you're the one who's going to have all the ideas, that's not going to happen. You have to get good people, trust them, and let them do their jobs. I'm collaborative and inclusive, a value in American Indian culture. Reciprocity, humbleness, humor, all of these qualities represent our values. You have to be willing not to be the smartest person in the room.

What impact did your family and upbringing have on your career path?

My dad is from southeastern Kentucky. His options growing up were to work in the coal mine or go into the service. My mother is from here, from St. Ignatius, and my parents met here. My mother went to the Catholic boarding school here on the reservation where she boarded until high school. She had that boarding school experience. Her mother was also boarded but in South Dakota.

She was adamant that the only way to impact your life, to make a huge change, was to go to college. She didn't see a lot of future here on the reservation. Things have changed here in the last 40 years. When she was here growing up, there were few options. She wanted us to have a lot of opportunity. It was an interesting discussion with my parents about going to college. They said, "You're going to college. We can't help you pay for it, we don't know how to get you in the [higher education] system, we can't navigate that, but you're going and you need to figure it out." It was that kind of "Will yourself through it," and all about them wanting a better future. I actually started taking some [college] classes in high school. I wasn't very happy about my high school experience because I couldn't shut off the disparities I saw; even though I was only in high school, you could still see them. Taking the classes at night my mom said, "I know you're not in love with high school," but I *was* in love with the classes I was taking in college. That set me on my path. I don't know if I would have graduated from high school otherwise. I took a dual enrollment program back in 1977 with Salish Kootenai College before the college had a campus. The classes were being offered through the college, which in turn, was helping (SKC) get formed. I took one evening class each quarter and just loved it! These classes made me decide, quite firmly, that I wanted more.

My dad is also American Indian but from Kentucky, "undocumented" we might say. His family, living through a time where crosses got burned in front yards, didn't discuss their affiliation fully or openly. It was very interesting when my dad married my mother; his family had a momentary panic because it was, "Oh my gosh. This is an Indian woman." That got resolved, but there were a few moments where it was unsure if matters would be okay. My mother was not white. To bring someone into my father's community who was not white and visibly American Indian could be problematic in Kentucky. Segregation of the late 50's and early 60's South was in full effect. The elementary school that I attended in first grade in Mississippi was just undergoing racial integration. This is the historical backdrop I refer to. My dad is white-passing, his whole family is. If you look at my dad's genealogy, it doesn't go very far back and then it's gone, buried.

What mentors or sponsors have had the greatest impact on your professional trajectory?

My parents, of course. I started working with Joe McDonald, SKC's founding president, when I was 19. He's 89 now. I got to watch how the early founders, Joe McDonald and Jerry Slater, worked together. I was part of that collaboration. They would share and talk about everything openly. There was a lot of mentoring that went on there. Later, I learned much from Bob Van Gouten, who worked here as well, about collaboration and administration. They encouraged and pushed everyone to dream bigger and envision how things could go farther than they ever thought. When you talk about this college and how it was formed, the founders just had this dream and no money, but they created life for this dream. Again, they willed it into being. Everyone had a piece to play in the building of this college. Much of the vision involved accepting challenge and risk to see what incredible transformations could happen.

You never get anywhere on your own. Wherever you are, you have people who came before you and people who will come after you along the journey. The idea of inclusion and collaboration, working together, is all about, "this isn't for me". I was given this gift by people who worked really hard before me. I need to build and take care of this campus and community for the people who will come after me. The "me" is our community, our collective. When I think about Salish Kootenai College, it's all of us who make up Salish Kootenai College. We wouldn't have what exists here without the students we serve and the faculty that we attract to work here. The faculty bring special characteristics because not everyone wants to work in this environment. The people serving our students in our student services area relate to and are connected to our community expectations. The college is about how to manage our tribal affairs. This college has a wide-reaching impact. People are really invested in how the college does, not just financially in terms of enrollment, but also in terms of how the people are here. The collective value of inclusion means making the community what we want it to be by reinvesting resources in our community and the tribal nations in general.

For example, if we teach people how to be authoritarian leaders, that's not going to play well in our tribal communities. We really try to infuse our cultural values and perspectives into all the classes and our business model. Our Tribal College serves students from approximately 60 different tribal nations. Each one has its own cultural values. We bring the cultural values and perspectives of our tribe into our practice. It also allows for the sharing of diverse tribal perspectives.

Doctoral degree attainment among American Indians is low.[2] What do you see as the biggest obstacles and most promising practices to help promote doctoral degree attainment among American Indians?

The biggest deterrent I see is the finances needed to complete a doctoral degree. The first thing is getting the funding piece in place. We find many American Indians tend to pursue those graduate degrees later in life; they might be doing it while they're working, or raising families, so the finances are a big thing. The other piece is that many are looking to advance their degrees to put them in a position to be able to better give back to their communities or stay where they're working.

One of the challenges I have here at the college in trying to increase the education attainment of many of my faculty is that Indian country doesn't pay the biggest wages. If a faculty member invests $40,000 in a doctoral program or $60,000, the chances of making that up in salary isn't going to happen. It's not being driven by your ability to make more money. The way that we have been successful in having faculty achieve those advance degrees is by finding funding for them, so that when they complete, they don't have these large debts that they're never going to be able to pay. Tribal college faculty typically earn an average of $50,000 per year and that's at the top end. There are some colleges, sad to say, that pay in the upper $30Ks or lower $40Ks. That's a difficult situation if you're trying to pay off graduate school debts.

We reach out to the American Indian College Fund which has some resources. We write grants to try to promote doctoral attainment and, we have fundraising efforts. Our college has just started two graduate programs here-a master's in education and a master's in natural resources. This came about because the community-in order to take on some of the tribal management we've stepped into-is now managing the national bisons' range, we have a hydro-electric dam, and we just got a water compact signed that requires a significantly higher level of training than our current folks have; the ones who have the training are at retirement age. We have to build that infrastructure and talent pipeline, so we created those programs to address these workforce needs. One of the ways we can help build degree attainment is through tuition waivers for some of our people to advance in the master's degree programs. If I have someone with a bachelor's who's interested in becoming a faculty member and earning a master's degree, we can help them, but we don't have a doctoral program. We need candidates with doctorates because if I retire in 10 years, I want to have people who are ready to take the helm.

Other promising practices include working with the University of Montana, 50 miles south of us, that has a number of doctoral programs they do in a cohort model. We've been able to encourage some people that way. We also have up to six hours of release time for faculty each week to pursue educational degrees or activities. However, the cost can still be prohibitive at a university and impact the ability to participate, so trying to break that financial barrier is truly one of the greatest obstacles. Almost anything else we can mitigate. People are place-bound; they're here because they want to be here, so if education opportunities present for them, few tend to leave afterwards. They have families here and tend to stay. SKC tends to pay more than most tribal colleges. We don't compete with the university and their wages. When we've done those competitive comparisons, we're in the lower range, but with inflation right now, that's not good.

Because we're very collaborative, we wear a lot of hats, our faculty do a lot of grant writing, and our students are high-touch students. We really integrate into the community and are very interactive with our students. For some people, they're not comfortable with that level of relationship, but that's what we must have for our students to succeed. Our funding is 65% funded through grants-there's a heavy grant load-and that's not for everybody either. However, if you like creativity, want some flexibility, and that student-relationship component, this is a place to thrive. We have just under 600 students.

What would you like readers to know about Salish Kootenai College and about the Tribal Colleges[3] in general?

The tribal colleges play a critical role in our communities. They help break the cycles of poverty. They help to set the direction for our tribal nations. We are sovereign nations within a nation. The tribes build their capacity as sovereign nations, and the tribal colleges help to build that vision of our tribes and where we want to go. Forty years ago when SKC formed, many of the positions in natural resources—many but not all— had people here from Boston or elsewhere who were managing the resources, but today most of the positions are filled by people from here because they got the education from SKC to fill those positions. We're making the decisions about our resources today, and that's a significant change. That's what Tribal Colleges do in their communities. We're training the social workers working with our social work department, we're creating more teachers to teach in our school districts. The people managing the water and operating all the business functions. Now that we're managing our own decisions for our own tribal people—that's because of the college.

I would like people to know that SKC is an amazing place! People in the community will tell you that SKC is like the jewel of the tribe. The college is the place where you can build and dream about the future you want to have.

What are you most proud of and is there anything you may have done differently along your path?

What I'm most proud of is the language and culture program work we're doing here at SKC. It took a long time and building a lot of relationships to do the deep language and culture work that we need to do. In our mission is to perpetuate the language and culture, not to preserve it, which means it needs to be living. The people who know it are only here for a finite amount of time. We've been able to create language and culture apprenticeships. That is the thing I'm most proud of. We do so much good in our nursing and other programs, but the language and culture is unique, our heart.

I struggle with what I would have done differently all the time because you only know what you know at the present, right? Sometimes when I wish I would have done some things differently, my husband reminds me that if I hadn't done what I did, I wouldn't be where I am. You never know what bullets you dodged or what opportunities you opened by the choice you made at a particular time. Would I have done anything differently? I probably would've spent a bit more time learning about budgets because I try to explain to people the college's budget every year, and it's very complex. I wish the work around building faculty around language and culture could have been implemented sooner at a fuller level, but it was funding-driven.

How has the 2020 racial reckoning and the pandemic impacted your leadership, students, and operations at Salish Kootenai College?

The pandemic shook up a lot. It's been tough. When you take a group of people who are very collaborative and relationship-driven and you isolate everybody, that's tough. We did what we had to do which was to try to normalize discussions around mental health and asking for help, not just for students but for everybody. We focused on providing for basic needs and trying to make the very best decisions we could at the time for the health and the well-being of the entire community. I'm glad we're slowly starting to come out of it. We lost a lot of people. The first round of Covid, we weren't impacted too heavily; a lot of the other reservations were. We thought everything was going to be good, but then we rolled into the second round and our reservation started experiencing deaths the second round. The first round we had maybe 20 people or so in isolation; the second round, we had over 100 either sick or in quarantine and providing services for all those people. We're back out of it and have maybe two people impacted, but we really had to make a decision as a community that we were going to take care of each other.

Navigating this whole rise in incivility, less than civil discourse, and open racism has been really interesting. While on campus, people have maintained expectations of how we interact. We have a set of agreements called "Our Way of Being" developed by our employees about six years ago. We think about how we respect each other's experiences and engage with one another i.e. that you don't have to agree, nor do you need to be antagonistic or caustic. Our community has seen a huge influx of people from the pandemic, the flight caused because we're a beautiful, rural place to live. This flight has created a huge problem in terms of housing. Right now, you cannot find a place to rent, and if you do, a 1-bedroom place that might have cost you $700 two years ago is $1300 now. The median price of a house in Missoula, 50 miles south of us, is now at $500,000 and higher than that if you go up to Kalispell. On the reservation, we're seeing an incredible number of houses in the $800K-$1 million range, which means that the person who lives here who tries to go to school here, that works here, is really struggling to find anywhere to live.

Communication around this is interesting because we're a "checker-boarded" reservation which means that when the allotments were done last in the 1800s, they actually sold every other interior lot to Southerners. When our reservation was established that way, it meant that it broke up some families and the cohesive structure of our reservation. We're the only one like this in Montana; there are others in the nation. We're also the only public law 638 tribe,[4] which means there is concurrent jurisdiction for legal services. Under the other reservations, legal matters are federal and tribal. However, here it's federal, tribal, state, everything, so when people move here, they tend to not understand that this is a reservation.

We manage certain resources for the future, not for the economic gain today. The way we take care of water, land, and air is different than if you bought somewhere else and went into an economic venture. We're going to look at whether there's colluding, high density, etc. As those different worldviews have connected with those who don't know anything about Indian people, it's been a little volatile. It looks smooth on the surface, but you don't have to dig very deep to see this discord. We've been navigating this scenario as we always have, but it's been magnified with the pandemic.

We tend to be located in pretty rural areas and tend to be pretty invisible to most of America. When you think about our population being less than a million people in the United States, when you start reading any of the demographic data on education, health, other factors, we are an asterisk. People aren't knowledgeable, and if they do know something, they often don't understand how tribes ended up where they are today and why things work the way they do. They tend to go to the race issue, but it's not a race issue, it's an issue of political status. It frames a lot of how these discussions happen. As the country has been talking more negatively about critical race, diversity, and inclusion, it's been interesting to watch how other higher education institutions want to address this by recruiting American Indian students to their campuses, and maybe they are or aren't prepared to support them. The discussion becomes about their initiatives, which may not necessarily be good for the communities, or they may not be having discussions with the communities themselves. This whole period of what's going on with voting and redistricting, all of those things when considering rural communities and reservations, they experience disproportionate impact. We tend to be congregated within particular areas intentionally.

Given the high number of women presidents and students in the Tribal College movement,[5] how would you encourage other American Indian women to pursue higher education leadership?

Many tribal communities are matriarchal. If you can think about a base tenet in tribal communities, leadership, and ceremony, it's all about the balance. What that means for women is that women bring a perspective, and men bring a perspective, and it's all about balance. Many American Indian women have opportunities to be leaders within the community as a parent, a cultural person, or as an educator which involves translating that commitment and vision of your community and leadership to a little bit of a higher level in education that's formal. There's a lot of informal positional leadership in the community.

In our higher education, it's about a goal-oriented leadership that's to help create the people we need for the future. If you think about women, that's not too much of a stretch. I often encourage women to own their gifts. Women like to self-deprecate; being boastful about yourself is not a good thing in Indian Country. There's a lot of stories about what happens if you get too full of yourself, but you can do this in a way that honors tradition. Being a leader does not mean you're always the one out front, it means how to bridge multiple pieces together. If you can work with women and in their experiences in mainstream schools and work environments, this is not always the message. Somewhere along the way, that confidence gets eroded. It becomes important to build a sense of confidence among women and remind women they know a lot, have done a lot, and ask them to call on their experience. The message becomes: "You can do this if you want to do this!"

This kind of work is critical. If you think of the 40 years of the Tribal College movement, it's new and we're still developing it. We're trying to create the people to give this gift to carry it forward. It's not like this movement and work has always been here. We have to tend it and care for it because we're still in that advocate/activist place for making higher education ours to serve us. Education was a weapon that was used against us. We're trying to turn that around and make education a tool of power for us.

We've been pretty successful. In higher education, the oldest tribal college is Diné, and they're just over 50 years old. We're babies in this whole thing.

What Can We Learn?

Dr. Boham emphasizes the importance of accepting opportunities that come along our career journeys whether or not they fit our pre-conceived idea of the "right" path to pursue. She also cites the importance of building a strong team who possess skills different from those she considers her strengths. She encourages women to move from self-deprecation to self-appreciation, building confidence, and establishing goals to help create the leaders of the future in Tribal Colleges and among the Tribal Nations.

Notes

1 The author asked Dr. Boham about terminology when referring to Native American/American Indian peoples.

   She says it best: "If you ask, you'll get all sorts of answers. I tend to use American Indian rather than Native American because that is the federal political status. That's why we have the Bureau of Indian Affairs. It's American Indian education, not Native American education in the actual laws and regulations. Mostly, you'll hear people want to be recognized by their tribal nation name. We're a confederacy here with three names."

2 Patel, V. (2014). Why so few American Indians earn PhDs, and what colleges can do about it. *Chronicle of Higher Education. Diversity in Academe.* https://www.purdue.edu/naecc/documents/2014%205-27%20 Why%20So%20Few%20American%20Indians%20Earn%20Ph.D.pdf.

   Shotten, H.T. (Fall 2018). Reciprocity and nation building in Native American women's doctoral education. *American Indian Quarterly, 42* (4), 488–507. https://www.jstor.org/stable/10.5250/amerindiquar.42.4.0488.

3 The idea for Indian colleges began around 1911.

   Crum (1989) argues that three developments in the 1960s led to the Tribal College consortium. These developments included the rise of Indian activism in the 1960s, socioeconomic reforms of the Great Society, and the concept of Indian self-determination which emerged in the 1960s and became policy in the 1970s.

   Crum, S. (1989). The idea of an Indian college or university in twentieth century America before the formation of the Navajo Community College in 1968. *Tribal College (1989–1989), 1*(1), 20.

   Crum (2007) also remarks that the tribal people of the 1960s were fully aware that higher education had never been encouraged for the vast majority of Native Americans by the dominant white society. To foster self-determination and affordable higher education opportunity, American Indians sought to create native run colleges. The Navajo Community College was the first Tribal College established in 1968 and was later renamed Diné College in 1997.

Crum, S. (2007). The Choctaw nation: Changing the appearance of American higher education, 1830–1907. *History of Education Quarterly, 47*(1), 49–68.

The American Indian Higher Education Consortium (AIHEC) formed in 1973 comprising the first six Tribal Colleges (TCUs). The AIHEC asserts that Tribal Colleges formed to respond to the higher education needs of American Indians and serve geographically isolated populations lacking access to post-secondary education. TCUs are public institutions of higher education, chartered by federally recognized Indian tribes with majority Native American or Alaska Native student enrollment, and funded through the federal Tribally Controlled Colleges and Universities Assistance Act of 1978. TCUs include two-year institutions, technical colleges offering certificates and associate degrees, and four-year colleges offering bachelor's and master's degrees. Today, the AIHEC recognizes 35 accredited Tribal Colleges serving approximately 15,200 students in 14 states.

American Indian Higher Education Consortium (2023). *About AIHEC: TRIBAL colleges: Educating, engaging, innovating, sustaining, honoring.* Aihec.org/who-we-are/index.htm.

4 638 authority is a tool that has been successful to increase Tribal control of programs and solutions being implemented in their communities. Public Law No. 93-638, 88 Statute 2203 (often referred to as 638 authority) gives Tribes the ability to manage certain programs that federal governments had previously administered through contracts and compacts. There are multiple options for what this can look like based on specific Tribal or regional needs.

Grogg, R., *A Primer on 638 Authority: Extending tribal self-determination to food and agriculture.* www.hungercenter.org/wp-content/uploads/2019/03/Shelli-Grogg-HFCR.pdf

5 Billy, C. (2019). The pathfinders: Women leaders in the tribal college movement. *Tribal College: Journal of American Indian Higher Education,30*(4),18–22.https://tribalcollegejournal.org/the-pathfinders-women-leaders-in-the-the-tribal-college-movement.

DATA USA: Tribal Colleges (2020). Enrollment. https://datausa.io/profile/university/tribal-colleges#:~:text=Students%20enrolled%20at%20Tribal%20Colleges%20in%20full%2Dtime%20Undergraduate%20programs,and%20White%20Female%20(5.53%25).

7

"Running Through the Fire"

Interview with Dr. Judy K. Sakaki

President Emeritus, Sonoma State University

Dr. Judy K. Sakaki[1] was appointed President of Sonoma State University in July 2016. She was the nation's first Japanese American woman to serve as president of a college or university where she served until July 2022. I became acquainted with Dr. Sakaki through the writing of this book.

A portion of this chapter was published in *Women in Higher Education* in March 2022.

Describe your job in one sentence.

I open doors, inspire, lead, serve, advocate, support my campus community, and transform lives.

How has your leadership style been shaped by being a first-generation college student and the first Japanese American woman to lead a college or university?

My leadership style is shaped by my experiences of the challenges that first-generation college students, women, and people of color face on college campuses and in life. People often have certain images of what a leader looks, sounds, or acts like. It is not just the responsibility of diverse

Women in the Higher Education C-Suite: Diverse Executive Profiles, First Edition. Lisa Mednick Takami.

leaders to adapt and develop leadership styles that fit expectations, but it's also the responsibility of others to broaden their understanding and acceptance of what leadership looks like.

What were the significant educational and professional steps in your career trajectory? How did previous positions prepare you to serve as President of Sonoma State University?

Early in my career, I was curious to learn how a university operated and how decisions impacting students were made. I got elected to serve on every committee within the Academic Senate on my campus. I learned so much that it encouraged me to pursue my doctoral degree...

My experiences serving as a vice president and vice chancellor for student affairs prepared me well to later serve as president of Sonoma State University. There is such a wide range of issues that you grapple with in student affairs. I worked with students and their parents, managed emergencies, created a strategic plan, assessed services, managed budgets, handled personnel issues, gave motivational speeches, inspired others to do their best and fundraised. Those experiences prepared and strengthened me to be an effective president.

In 2017, you lost your home in the California Tubbs Fire. How did you cope with this personal loss while continuing to fulfill your duties as president?

Not only did I lose my home and every single thing I owned, but I also almost lost my life... I never in my worst nightmare could have imagined this, yet somehow, I mustered the strength to run...

We were so fortunate that just when my husband and I thought we wouldn't survive, an off-duty firefighter found us and saved our lives. We're forever changed by this horrific life experience.

What was amazing was the care and the wonderful support from members of the campus community and total strangers. That is one of the signatures of Sonoma State. We had 80 faculty, staff and students who also lost their homes. We created a program and got laptops, books, and clothes for fire victims... I was living in one of our residence hall apartments. I knew all eyes were on me, and I could not fall apart. As a president and a community leader, I needed to step up and demonstrate that we could go on...

We have a beautiful performing arts center on campus, and community members suggested we hold a fundraiser for first responders. I thought

long and hard about being a role model and the responsibility that comes with leadership. I spoke about how difficult it was and how important it was to go for counseling to heal.

Under your leadership, Sonoma State saw a significant increase in the 4-year graduation rate and the 2-year graduation rate for transfer students.[2] How did you and your teams work to improve student outcomes given your emphasis on access, affordability, inclusion, and success?

I believe in the strength of teams. When I came to Sonoma State, I was interested in creating a student-centered community. It didn't matter what your job was—a grounds person, a food service worker, an advisor,

or a dean—how we show up makes a difference in the lives of students...
If everyone has this sense of student-centered responsibility, then we lift
our students and our campus...

We also created structures—we have a transfer and transition center,
beefed up our advising, reach[ed] out more intentionally to students and
[made] sure we have classes that support students at times they want
them.

*You have noted the importance of "lifting as you rise" and the few role
models available as you developed your career. What mentors or
sponsors had the most impact on your professional development? How
do you prioritize mentoring?*

I did not have any mentors who looked like me. I found there were
many people who may not look like me, but who would care and provide
support. Things are changing slowly in the academy in terms of role
models. The number of women presidents and chancellors is still about
30% and changing little. The number of women presidents of color is even
fewer.

When I receive a request from a doctoral, master's or undergraduate
student to mentor, I accept. I also chair the American Council on
Education Women's Network. We're creating a pilot mentoring program.
For all who may think, "I don't know if I should go for that position," I
would say, "Just try it, go for it." Listen to your mentors and others who
may see something in you that you don't yet see in yourself.

*You've remarked on how implicit bias regarding your Japanese
background surfaced during your career. How did bias show up and what
did you do to confront it?*

I have experienced implicit bias and overt racism at every step of my
career. It's hurtful. When people say, "Why are there so few Asian
American women in these leadership roles?" I smile and could say, "Do
you want to see the scars on my back?" I maintain that if I were six feet tall
and male, I don't think they'd ask me that question. We still have that bias
and the stereotyping that makes it harder to excel in these leadership
positions...

For a long time, I tried to be the role models I saw—white women. I'd
see this assertion, this aggression... that was not my personality. I thought
if I aspired to be a leader, I needed to be more like them.

Early in my career, I went to lunch with the then Chair of the Academic Senate and told her that I'd been watching her because I wanted to be more like her. She said: "Judy, that's really interesting because I've been watching you and want to be more like you." I couldn't imagine this. [She said] "You don't speak as often as I do, but when you speak, people listen to you... and when you go into a meeting, you know what you want and you don't leave until you get it." Later in my career I said to myself, "This is who I am, right? I can be an effective leader with these skills, this personality, these cultural values, and traits."

What impact did your family and upbringing have on your career trajectory?

So many Japanese traits come to mind such as, "gaman", to just tough it out. This came out of the internment also, "shikata ga nai", some things just can't be helped. Pivotal values have helped me, this perseverance, this strength. My mother and father used to say, "Tsumoreba yama to naru." The translation is, "Even the tiniest particles of dust, when you gather them together, can create a mountain that enables others to climb higher and see farther than you ever dreamed possible." ... These sayings have stuck with me.

How did you address combatting anti-Asian hate among anti-racist instances at Sonoma State University?

The president of Santa Rosa Junior College is a Chinese American man, and the superintendent of the Santa Rosa public schools is a Japanese American woman. Together as Asian American leaders, we wrote an op-ed piece for the *Press Democrat* about how anti-Asian hate and racism had impacted our lives. On campus we created, "Brave Spaces," and town hall meetings where people could come together... I participated and communicated to the campus community... creating an awareness, being that role model [and] creating spaces on campus for people to ask questions or be with each other in community.

When I'm walking around off-campus, I'm not the president of the university, I'm just an Asian American woman. All the issues of race and our racial reckoning in this country have raised these issues... We need to educate each other.

An alum once left a hateful voice message with many derogatory comments which said, "I will never give a penny to a 'J-p from an internment camp.'" It was distressing and felt very threatening. I felt that we didn't do a good job of educating this person if he's out in the world saying these kinds of things... I go back to that Japanese saying, "tsumoraba yama to naru," every little thing we do can help create that mountain that will make us better... We're about educating and lifting students to understand difference and learn from each other.

What would you recommend to readers interested in pursuing a CEO role in higher education?

Go for it, prepare yourself, and follow advice. Get several mentors, shadow people [and] think seriously about what you're less comfortable doing... Whether it's making your way around a room, or speaking in front of 100, 500 or 1,000 people, get comfortable doing it.... Push yourself out of your comfort zone... Be strong and stay flexible so that you can bend and adapt...[to] challenging, sometimes unpredictable circumstances.

Author's Note: Dr. Sakaki stepped down from her role as President of Sonoma State University in July 2022. Dr. Sakaki retired and was named President Emeritus of Sonoma State. She serves as Professor of Educational Leadership at California State University, East Bay, in their Educational Leadership for Social Justice Doctoral program.

What is your perspective on the events that took place leading to your stepping down as President of Sonoma State University in July 2022?

The comments below are those I made at the California State University Chancellor's Senior Leadership Council (CSLC) Zoom Meeting on August 16, 2022. The CSLC comprises the presidents of the 23 California State University campuses, the six senior administrators at the Chancellor's Office, and the Chancellor:

> "I'd like to open with something a faculty member sent to me, a poem by Mark Nepo called *The Instruments of Change*.[3]

'The storm is not as important as the path it opens. The mistreatment in one life never is as crucial as the clearing it makes in your heart. This is very hard to accept. The hammer or cruel one is always short-lived compared to the jewel in the center of the stone.'

A Sonoma State faculty member wrote this in a note that said, 'From the fires, to your latest challenges, the bamboo rises. May you be blessed with renewal and abundance. In a world growing darker, you are such a model of how to move through the challenges of life.'"

I expressed to this group that I was grateful for the words of support and appreciation for my leadership that they had expressed, before I spoke, and the opportunity that I had to lead Sonoma State University for six years. I always told students, faculty, and others that they should work to leave their campus better than it was when they arrived. I am proud of changing the campus culture to become more student-centered, to have diversified the student body and the faculty, to have improved our Graduation Initiative measures, and to have brought more community engagement with the campus.

My public remarks continued, "But the last three to four months have been harder for me than running barefoot uphill through the wildfires for my life. Just one year into my presidency, I lost my home, car, everything I owned and nearly my life. This latest experience has been harder for me than that experience, and that says a lot. I appreciate those that believed and supported me, but many, many were bystanders in a complex, difficult situation."

"Many asked me repeatedly to refute and tell my truth, but my culture, my personality, the advice I received from attorneys, my upbringing, my embarrassment precluded that. I really lost my voice. Plus, some stories I would have told, while all true, would have hurt Sonoma State, would have damaged the California State University (CSU), and would have hurt public higher education. I am a product of the CSU and public higher education, and I couldn't see doing this—it would have hurt us reputationally with donors, the public, and with legislators in Sacramento."

"I hope that as we embrace diversity in the system and in higher education that we also embrace diversity of leadership and leadership styles that includes gender and ethnic differences. I hope that none of you, other presidents, chancellors, or senior administrators, has to experience the humiliation, the attacks, the hurt that I have."

"So, what's next for me? I'm still serving on the American Council of Education's (ACE) board and on the ACE's Women's Network Executive Council. I am an appointed WASC (Western Association of Schools and Colleges) commissioner and an Asian Pacific Americans in Higher Education (APAHE) emeriti board member. I will continue with these leadership and service roles. In addition, I am a tenured professor in the School of Education, and I may choose to teach or work on special projects there. I'm giving myself a year to heal and decide on my next involvements."

I closed my comments to my colleagues with a Melody Beattie quote about gratitude:

Gratitude unlocks the fullness of life. It turns what we have into enough and more. It turns denial into acceptance, chaos to order, confusion into clarity. Gratitude makes sense of our past, brings peace for today and creates a vision for tomorrow.[4]

"It is with gratitude and best wishes to all of you that I close."

I received so much positive feedback for being honest in that Zoom meeting and situation. What was so hard was that no one said or did anything publicly through the months of attacks. That included women and men. Many women colleagues, community leaders, and friends expressed their support and urged me to persevere, but they did it privately by phone, text, email or cards and letters. Largely, men were silent. For me, the attacks felt relentless. They were coming from the media, the Chancellor's Office, faculty, and even elected officials.

Several women presidents texted me during my remarks at CSLC and afterwards, thanked me for what I had said, indicated I was the only person that they felt had been truly honest and had made a lot of people think, even people who didn't want to think about what had happened. One colleague texted, "I just want to say...you are an amazing warrior. You have always been a warrior but today what you said was so powerful. Just know that I appreciate everything that you have done. You were and still are an incredible role model, leader, and president. Everyone heard, respects and understood what you said. I, and many others, will miss you at the table."

Early in my career, I worked at a shelter for women who had been abused. This was the closest I had felt to their experiences, a sense of relentless battering, and I lost my voice. I couldn't fight back. It was so hard. What started out as a difficult personnel issue just grew.

I have a binder of support letters, but many wanted to offer support privately. And yet, there was all this loud opposition, mostly white males, just pouncing and going to the media on everything. The women leaders in this community, many who are major donors in the area, wrote me amazing supportive letters, but they didn't want to come out publicly. It was good to have emotional support, but I was distraught and exhausted and needed people to come out loud and push back and contact the Chancellor's Office and the Board and politicians, but I wasn't strong enough at that time to mobilize that.

Considering the issue of gender, how do you believe what unfolded may have evolved differently had you been a man in the same circumstances?

I know things would have evolved differently if I were a male president. I believe women presidents face a harsher reaction than male presidents when they must make tough personnel or other controversial decisions. I see my male counterparts who have had multiple votes of no-confidence, significant ones; mine was 175–105, and only 37% of the eligible faculty even voted. Yet the headline was, "Sakaki loses vote of no-confidence." These other men even had male trustees go to their campuses and defend them with multiple votes of no-confidence, and they're still sitting in their positions. Where is the equity, justice, and fairness for women?

We've come a long way, but we still clearly have farther to go. That's why I sit on the ACE's Women's Network Executive Council, and we talk about the need to still "move the needle." There still are not the numbers of women in senior administrative and president/chancellor positions, and when they are selected, as a CSU presidential colleague recently noted, Asian American presidents are in the lowest tier leading the smallest campuses with the lowest salaries.

I believe that as an Asian American woman president, I was treated differently than if I were white and/or male. I was asked if I was married when I was offered the job of president by the then Chancellor. I felt there was a total lack of support when my house burned down, and I had nowhere to live. About half of the CSU presidents reside in campus-owned homes.

Sonoma State did not have a presidential residence, but instead I received a $5,000 per month housing allowance. Over 5,000 homes burned in the Tubbs fire and housing in Sonoma County was scarce. We had to move six times in the year after the fire. When I asked for advice and assistance, the then Chancellor told me that maybe I just needed to move farther away and commute 1–2 hours, if needed. Because vision problems precluded my driving at night, I ended up having to rent a 3-bedroom ranch style home for $16,000 per month with no additional assistance from the Chancellor's Office. I believe that the male presidents experienced more camaraderie and hence received more support from the then Chancellor than I did.

The standards and expectations of what presidential spouses are supposed to do and be also differs between men and women spouses. I was told that when there were primarily male presidents and there were presidential retreats, the spouses would go off and go shopping. Some women presidents had husbands or partners who had careers of their own, and this changed the dynamic at some sessions. Not everyone was comfortable with this.

How can other women leaders and prospective women CEOs learn from your recent experiences?

Be strong. Be resilient. Expect the unexpected. Anticipate that challenging, difficult situations will occur. I trusted advice I was given internally, but if you work in a higher education system, the system is the client, not you. I learned that you could get thrown under the bus in a flash, irrespective of what you were previously told. By nature, I trust, I'm a trusting person. I believe people. Some say I'm too naïve. I now believe that you should hire and retain your own attorney for advice and counsel, just in case.

As Dr. Sakaki continues, "My remarkable and previously stellar career and reputation was upended by a mistake that I made in hiring one key senior administrator on my leadership team. I believe that teams are stronger when there is diversity of backgrounds, disciplines, and experiences. Yet, in this one case, I went against my own instincts, my gut, for the first time and allowed myself to be persuaded by others. This error in judgment and failure to heed my own perceptions will forever be a regret."

Early in my career when I was an ACE Fellow, I went to CSU Northridge right after the major 1994 earthquake. Dr. Blenda Wilson was the president at the time, one of the first African American women presidents in the country. When I asked for advice as I thought about an administrative career, she said that if I aspired or rose to a senior administrative level, I should have two houses. I was young and didn't understand so I asked her why. She responded that at some time, I would be blamed for something, or my integrity would not allow me to continue. "You will want to leave town as fast as you can and having a second home will allow you to do that." I didn't understand this early in my career, but I remembered it all these years. Now I get it.

How did you reach the difficult decision(s) regarding your marriage?

It's still in process. We're a relatively new couple. What we were going through was horrendous. I was being attacked; he was being attacked. We have different cultural and family backgrounds. He's a lobbyist, and he saw and experienced things differently than I did. He'd seen the lack of integrity, the evil, that I didn't want to see. I couldn't see it. He got really incensed and outraged, and he didn't fully understand the 'Japaneseness' in me. It's been horrific, sad, and horrendous, personally and professionally.

From the day I started as president, my husband was at every dinner helping me fundraise, he was beside me lending support. To get attacked with falsehoods about how he interacted with people was so hurtful. He felt that I didn't defend him enough. I was drowning. It was clear that much of what got leaked in that first, horrendous *Los Angeles Times* article was a 28-page brief that had confidential information, for settlement purposes only, of attorney-client privileged information. My husband was livid and could see the damage to both of our reputations and careers. In his anger he sent an email that he should not have sent.

While I had no knowledge beforehand of it, the information in the email that he sent to 'family and friends' was honest. Although he did not intend for his email to be distributed, it somehow found its way to the media and was published. I was strongly advised to disassociate myself from him and his email to try to salvage my presidency. A press statement was written and released that severely damaged our marriage. This whole situation was so out of control and is almost still beyond my comprehension. I wonder if a female spouse of a male president who took similar actions would be treated and held accountable in the same manner?

My husband and I have been through a lot together, including having Post Traumatic Stress Disorder (PTSD) from the fires. Initially, I couldn't sleep because every time I closed my eyes, I could see flames and feel the intense heat. In hindsight, I was plowing ahead just one year into my presidency and didn't think I should take any time off. We had nothing after the fires, not even shoes. We were dealing with the insurance companies and trying to figure out where we were going to live. It was a lot to manage, and we both had our careers. My husband was working in Sacramento, and we were living apart during the week then and trying to cope. When I think back on the time of the wildfires, if we hadn't had one another, I don't think either of us would have survived running through the inferno or the aftermath. It was all unimaginably horrific.

We're now trying to understand all that has happened and how each of us could have, should have, or would have done things differently. We cannot change all that has happened as much as we might wish we could. But we can gain insight with compassion and forgiveness for ourselves, each other, and for others that can help us to heal and grow.

What would you like your legacy to be?

Across the span of over 44 years in public higher education in California, I have improved access, affordability, and student success for hundreds of thousands of students, especially low- income and students of color. I improved the lives and futures of many students and their families.

In addition, I have improved support services including mental health services and services for undocumented, veterans, disabled and other targeted groups. I accomplished changes in policies and practices on several CSU and UC campuses where I served as Vice President/Vice Chancellor for Student Affairs.

I also led changes in admissions and student support services across the University of California system where I served as Vice President of the UC system. One of my proudest accomplishments was orchestrating the awarding of honorary degrees to Japanese Americans who were UC students but were unable to complete their degrees because they were sent to Internment camps. It took an affirmative vote by each of the 10 campus academic senates and a unanimous vote of the Regents to accomplish this goal despite a 29-year moratorium on the awarding of honorary degrees and an unsupportive then president.

I began my career in higher education as an outreach counselor and then became an Educational Opportunity Program and Summer Bridge Program director opening the doors of opportunity for hundreds of new college students who were the first in their families to go to college.

I am proud to have been the first Japanese American woman president of a 4-year university in the country. As president of Sonoma State, I radically changed the culture of the campus to be focused on student success. I made the campus more diverse and inclusive. When I arrived as president, I inherited a leadership team that was all male and lacking in diversity. I changed and modeled the benefits of equity, diversity, and inclusion across the campus. I redirected resources to academic and student affairs and turned the Green Music Center into a performing arts center for the entire campus and community with an Arts Integration Program for students and moved Commencement ceremonies into this world-class facility.

The campus survived the wildfires but 80 faculty, staff, and students like me lost their homes. Two weeks after the fire, we reopened the campus with a "Gratitude Gathering", and with a Noma Cares campaign, we helped fire victims replace books, laptops, and other essentials so that they could all resume their studies or work.

I was a first-gen college student. My parents were sent to the Japanese American Internment Camps. They didn't have the chance to go to college. I became a single parent, my kids were three and five at the time, and I worked full-time and completed my PhD at UC Berkeley. I hope that one of my legacies is to continue to be a role model and to encourage others, especially women and people of color, to hang onto their dreams. My parents used to say in Japanese "Gambatte" and "Chikara" encouraging me to always do my best, to never give up and to stay strong.

Everyone is going to hit bumps in the road during their lives and careers. I never expected to be a single mom of two sons. I never expected to lose my home and all my possessions in a fire. And I certainly never expected the racism, sexism, mean-spiritedness and lack of support during my presidency. But one has to remain self-confident, true to one's values with integrity, grace and resilience.

Remembering my "obaachan" or grandmother–an immigrant picture bride who faced incredible discrimination and untenable circumstances and yet remained optimistic and grateful–helps to pull me through my challenging times. I made my mark whether it was at the University of California, Office of the President, at UC Davis, in the CSU, Chancellor's Office, at CSU East Bay, Fresno State, or Sonoma State.

I always led with integrity, had a strong work ethic, was a person of my word, cared deeply about students, faculty, staff, was a strong advocate for public higher education, a role model for women and people of color, and a caring mentor to many. Implicit and explicit bias in higher education and society is real. Unfortunately, I have experienced the double whammy of both racism and sexism throughout my 40+ year career. I am proud of my contributions and all that I have accomplished. I still believe deeply in the power of education to lift individuals, families, communities, and society. We still have much work to do.

What Can We Learn?

Dr. Sakaki's personal and professional narrative highlights a cautionary tale for prospective women presidents, particularly women of color who may be vulnerable to experiencing the dual marginality of racism and sexism. Dr. Sakaki's strong ties to her Japanese ancestry and values of hard work, ambition, integrity, and resilience helped her thrive, while she also acknowledges that her cultural background challenged her to maintain her voice and agency when she most needed it. Through organizations like the American Council on Education's Executive Women's Council, aspiring women CEOs can learn with and from other women facing common challenges. Cultivating trusted mentors to help shepherd leaders through troubling times appears key.

Notes

1 Dr. Sakaki's middle initial "K" stands for Kaoru, a name connected to her paternal grandmother, Shigeru Sakaki. The grandmother she refers to in her interview is her maternal grandmother Konoye Hirota. https://www.immigrant-voices.aiisf.org/stories-by-author/konoye-hirotas-journey-inspires-generations/.

2 North Bay Leadership Council (2022). https://northbayleadership.org/judy-sakaki.

Joyner, A. (2021). Leadership and lived experience: Q&A with Dr. Judy Sakaki, president of Sonoma State University. *Diverse Issues in Higher Education.* https://www.diverseeducation.com/institutions/hbcus/article/15098133/judy-k-sakaki.

3 Nepo, M. (2004). *"Fighting the Instrument"* in *Suite for the Living*. Novato, CA: Bread for the Journey International.

4 Gratitude. *Melody Beattie Daily Meditations.* https://melodybeattie.com/gratitude-2.

8

"The Wind of the Ancestors was at My Back"

Interview with Dr. Becky R. Petitt

Vice Chancellor for Equity, Diversity, and Inclusion, University of California, San Diego

Dr. Becky R. Petitt has served as the Vice Chancellor for Equity, Diversity and Inclusion at the University of California, San Diego since March 2015. UC San Diego is a public research university serving 22,700 undergraduate and 6,300 graduate students. I became acquainted with Dr. Petitt through my doctoral research on higher education chief diversity officers.

A portion of this chapter originally appeared in *Women in Higher Education* in April 2018.

Please describe your job in one sentence.

My job is to help create the most ideal teaching and learning environments for all our students, faculty, and staff.

Women in the Higher Education C-Suite: Diverse Executive Profiles, First Edition.
Lisa Mednick Takami.
© 2024 John Wiley & Sons, Inc. Published 2024 by John Wiley & Sons, Inc.

You previously served at Texas A&M University. What are some of the inherent challenges and opportunities in serving as a chief diversity officer (CDO) at UC San Diego?

I work to ensure that everybody who chooses to study or work at UCSD can thrive and that the teaching and learning environment is optimal for all. If people devote their mental or emotional resources to protecting themselves from assault or offense, they're not free to express their brilliance. While UCSD and Texas A&M have very different student demographics, both states have legislation that ostensibly makes it more challenging to pursue diversity. This legislation challenges educational equity because we don't all start from the same place. At both institutions, challenges and opportunities are more alike than they are dissimilar.

In general, when we advocate for greater inclusion, individuals perceive it as a force that may displace them somehow. At Texas A&M University, it took nearly 10 years for our diversity plan to take root and be a game changer. It may be the same at UCSD. While I'd like to accelerate the pace of change, it's important that I work at the pace that the organization can handle. It's a balance between demonstrating urgency and intentionally building coalitions to enable the change we need. I have to figure out how to go with the grain and make sure I take the time to engage people and help them understand how we all benefit from more inclusion while taking the temperature of the institution.

I've heard you discuss the importance of integrated and strategic diversity work and the role of senior campus leadership. Please elaborate.

I've seen equity, diversity, and inclusion efforts work, and I've paid attention to institutions where people in positions like mine have not been successful. One of the strategic mistakes made is when chief diversity officers (CDOs) are not properly introduced to the academic community. When I was hired, I asked the chancellor to convey to every unit leader that they should each consider the CDO as part of their leadership and decision-making teams. What I meant is that for every leadership decision, for every institution-level decision, people should be thinking about the impact on equity, diversity, and inclusion. For example, when a strategic decision is being undertaken, is an impact analysis being conducted? Together, let's ensure that this decision and all possible outcomes have been thoughtfully considered. Equity, diversity, and inclusion should be integrated into every operation of the institution. When we are establishing completion criteria or time-to-degree

expectations, we should be thoughtful about how that might impact various groups of students (e.g., those who work or those who want to retake a course for their own edification or for a better grade).

What was your educational and career path leading to your appointment as UC San Diego's vice chancellor of equity, diversity, and inclusion?

My baccalaureate is in psychology and my master's and PhD degrees are in higher education. Three things summarize my approach: (1) understanding people want to be seen, heard and valued and to live and work in an environment where they can do their best work and be the best version of themselves; (2) thinking about constituents who care about our mission, what it means to serve the public good and how higher education works; and (3) considering how to shift the culture of a large organization. Texas A&M is nearly twice the size of UC San Diego, but it's the culture not the size that matters, and the openness to change that counts. I often use the Peter Drucker quote "Culture eats strategy for breakfast." Regardless of the strategy I use, what counts is, have I really taken the time to understand this organization, to understand what matters and moves people, and invested time in learning how to work within the structure?

What impact did your family and upbringing have on your career choice as a chief diversity officer?

My father instilled the values of hard work and being ethical, and my mother was an activist and my deaf brother's chief advocate. My mom helped me understand true inclusion and what it means to make sure there is room at the table for everyone. Combining the value of hard work with the model of inclusion are important lessons that have stuck with me. My brother didn't want to go to a different school from the rest of his siblings, so my mother fought on my brother's behalf to be included. She worked at a structural level to improve the quality of education not just for my brother, but also for other people who came after him. In so many ways, I'm following in my mom's footsteps. I'm working for people at UCSD today, but also considering what it means to be an equitable and inclusive institution and removing barriers so the challenges of today are not the same years from now.

Which individuals or mentors have had the greatest impact on your professional development?

Dr. Damon A. Williams found a way to elevate the profession and put into the literature some of the important messages that helped not only professionalize our field, but also add to the body of knowledge. I feel honored to consider Damon one of my dear friends and thought colleagues. Also, I have deep respect for white allies. In my experience, there are white allies who say the right things and those who do the right things when the time calls for them to be courageous and step up. One of the things we must understand is that we need each other. Many CDOs are people of color. Just like in the many civil rights movements, we need allies to stand up and stand beside us when it matters. I have deep appreciation for white allies who show up when it really counts, and when they are not afraid to publicly demonstrate their solidarity. Finally, there is one person who told me I would never be a chief diversity officer. That person really strengthened my resolve to prove this person wrong. I value and appreciate people who believe in me and who have supported and encouraged me, but I'm also grateful to that individual who helped me to find my inner strength and do what I knew I could do.

What would you recommend to readers interested in pursuing a career as a chief diversity officer?

I think it's important to read broadly. There is something to learn from various disciplines. I enjoyed reading Atul Gawande's book, *Better: A Surgeon's Notes on Performance.*[1] I love this book because it examines optimizing organizational performance and being a "positive deviant"—using uncommon but successful strategies to facilitate better solutions. The chapter that stands out most is "On Washing Hands": Infection control specialists learned that doctors were spreading infections from patient to patient because, in a rush, they were not washing their hands before and after each patient. It's an interesting chapter about what it took to change the culture in a life-or-death situation. The answer was simple: Ask the doctors and engage the whole team in identifying solutions. We must ask and engage those most directly involved in decisions what will help them to perform better.

What would you like your legacy to be at UC San Diego?

I'd like it to be said that my team and I were able to create a more welcoming, more inclusive, more vibrant community and that we encouraged people to take accountability seriously.

Author's Note: An updated interview was conducted with Dr. Petitt in April 2022.

You have served as Vice Chancellor for Equity, Diversity, and Inclusion at UC San Diego since 2015. What have you learned about strategic diversity leadership and yourself over the past seven years?

Lived politics are different from perceived politics. There is more blatant prejudice, discrimination, and racial hostility in the southern part of the United States, and it makes its way onto college campuses because we are a microcosm of society. In California, liberal political views can obscure resistance to real DEIA change. I have fostered amazing collaborators, co-conspirators, and partners in progress that took time to grow.

In my current role, I have learned that operating under the radar somewhat allows me to be more successful. Rather than announcing strategies in advance, I find the partners needed, pursue the consultation process, and partner to get the work done to rebuild in a more equitable way. Though disagreement is useful, and it helps to listen to and respond to concerns, sometimes I take the path of least resistance. I take the time to find and build coalitions versus starting with the most intransigent. I have been successful in building things to last that will outlast me. Building relationships with people and working with them to co-create something that is more inclusive is critical to my success.

I prefer to engage my white colleagues as partners, a conscious, strategic choice. The anti-racist work we must do is the job of white people. Who better to help with this work than white men who have a receptive audience to the messages? In partnering with white, male faculty, I consider Audre Lorde who said, "The master's tools will never dismantle the master's house."[2], but in this work, we use the master's tools to dismantle structures and rebuild something more inclusive for all, and sometimes I add new tools to the toolbox. How do we make room for more voices? By getting white people to talk to their white colleagues to undo systems they created to exclude. It is important for me to partner with white colleagues and to position them to exercise their privilege to create space for all.

How have you led through the #MeToo, #StopAAPIHate, and #BlackLivesMatter movements, and the racial uprising of summer 2020?

Among these national, public events, none affected me as much as the summer uprisings of 2020.

Initially, reporting increased for sexual harassment relative to historic reporting. In working with my partners who investigate sexual harassment and were alarmed by the increase, I framed the development institutionally as a *positive* change. When people are comfortable coming forward to report, the problem is in the public arena and discourse, and we can get aggressive about emphasizing zero tolerance and addressing solutions.

The pain impacting our Asian American community, given the significant uptick in violence during the pandemic, proved difficult because we were operating remotely. We provided direct support, community support, and education through webinars and focus group discussions inviting our counseling and care teams to talk with and support out students. Webinars invited experts to discuss the issues our students and their loved ones were experiencing. We planned and executed educational events such as a seminar focused on Asian Americans, Desi Americans, and Pacific Asian Islander (APIMEDA) students in order to center their lived experiences. We reminded the larger community that our Asian American students are not a monolith; students and employees have unique experiences we need to be attentive to. These programs were supported by campus-wide messaging.

The hardest part for me was the uprisings that arose from repeated police brutality against black people because they hit home. I was in shock, and it is still difficult for me to discuss. Complicating matters, I received scrutiny that I was not doing enough to address the pain Black people were experiencing during this time. I was in pain, too. A distant relative of mine was killed by an off-duty police officer, and I have dark-skinned men in my family whose lives I am afraid for. My brother is deaf. I thought, "I can't protect him." Literally, if my brother were approached by a police officer who said, "Stop!", and he could not hear their commands, would I lose my brother? I worry about my family and about myself because I do not accept nor tolerate disrespect. If someone said something offensive to me, or threatened me, would I forget all I have to lose in that moment and speak or act before responding to the offense? Would I make it out alive from an altercation? I know the intense pain of *not* responding to indignity because you fear for your life. That reality is excruciating. My freedom, liberty, and right to live a full life, free of terror, is precarious.

Leading through this time with hope and not showing up broken when I felt broken took a great deal out of me. During the day, I showed up to help people understand that we would get to the other side. At night, there were many tears shed. As much as I did not want to show up at work crying, there were times when tears simply rolled down my face.

We modified a concept created by Dr. Eddie Moore, Jr. (known for the White Privilege Conference) built on the premise that it takes 21-days to learn a habit. We held a 21-day Anti-Racism Challenge. Our approach was that it takes 21-days to become educated on anti-racist practice. We divided anti-racism work into modules by doing readings, watching videos, and having invited guests discuss the readings and engage the audience. Thousands of participants took part. At one session, 8,000 people participated! I had a great team of colleagues co-leading this effort.

We initiated the 21-Day Antiracism Challenge[3] around the same time we received Black student demands. Some of our students complained that this initiative distracted from or ignored their demands. I had to help them realize that we are one community, and that faculty and staff need attention, support, and education too. Also, faculty and staff well-being and education help to create a better campus environment *for* our students. It is frustrating that people do not assume good intent or ask questions and that they are so quick to publicly criticize.

The period following summer 2020 compares to one of the most difficult situations I have ever faced as an administrator: Losing 12 students in a bonfire collapse at Texas A&M University. I was among administrators to meet with parents; a student victim's father collapsed in my arms as he wept. Like the summer of 2020, I had to lead in Texas while I felt broken. Looking back at the post-summer 2020 period, I wasn't broken at all, but I certainly felt that way. I'm just gaining clarity now about how

I led during that time. As we experienced the pandemic, people also thanked me for centering and prioritizing the needs of the most vulnerable and conducting an impact analysis for any decisions made. For example, we reached out to local underrepresented communities realizing that our institutional boundaries are fuzzy. Impact analyses have become a signature of my leadership approach. We are one community, and we need to take care of those on and off campus. We had on-campus vaccine availability and our mobile van offered COVID-19 vaccinations in the local community, with a focus on those most marginalized.

Looking back on that time, I would describe it as a period of operating in a state of shock and putting one foot in front of the other. My decisions were reasoned, thoughtful, and perhaps brilliant based on feedback I received. I wonder now, "how in the world did I do that?". The impact for me as a Black woman was rough. I compartmentalized, and the wind of the Ancestors was at my back. I relied on a network of good friends. Having a brave, supportive partner, good friends, and deep faith sustained me.

How has the pandemic impacted your work as a chief diversity officer and what changes implemented during the pandemic will be sustained at UC San Diego?

We wondered why we hadn't done some things earlier. While there's something special about being on campus, we learned we can create conditions for education to be accessible even if we're not physically present. Some members of our campus community fought against remote teaching and working until we had to shift. Faculty adjusted and realized they could deliver content online and students continued to learn. Some supervisors also resisted team members' working from home. However, remote work helped with business continuity, and it also helped new parents and those who had other caregiving responsibilities. Remaining attentive to the learning loss that has occurred through the pandemic is also important. Students coming to UC San Diego may have spent a year or more of high school learning from home. There was also an impact on social skills.

I would like us to remember how we teach students attending UC San Diego. We're a high-performing institution, and we continue to see record numbers of diverse applicants. We no longer require SAT or ACT scores for admission. Given this change and the pandemic's impacts, we need to listen to students given our responsibility to teach those who come to UC San Diego. The mark of a good faculty member and educator is their ability to teach any student and meet a student wherever they are when they begin here. Student learning is our responsibility. Educators' focus on teaching "the best of the best" is simply not enough. Realizing students' brilliance, their potential, and tapping into what students bring to the learning environment is critical.

You take an active role in training the next generation of chief diversity officers. How do you think the CDO role has changed in the last 10 years?

I'm excited that our area of work has become more professionalized. Dr. Damon Williams was one of the first to capture and articulate CDO work.[4] More literature on CDO work now exists, and doctoral students have written their dissertations on the CDO role.[5] Standards for the profession emerged about five years ago.[6] Over the last 10 years, we have created structure around what we do (e.g., strategic diversity plans, EDI units) as a profession, and CDO work is better understood.

Since the uprising of 2020, many institutions have created CDO roles in higher education, non-profits, Silicon Valley companies, and other private sector organizations.[7] However, some of these CDOs have been hired as window-dressing. The positions created are not situated so the CDOs have real authority. Some professionals in these roles are not positioned to be effective, and my concern is sustainability. For those who may *not* have the requisite knowledge, skills, and ability to do the job, there exists a myth that everyone can do equity, diversity, and inclusion work. Some of the people being recruited are learning on the job. I'm concerned that ten years from now the question will be asked, "Have these positions really made a difference?" I welcome that many other institutions are creating these positions. However, the positions must be set up so the CDOs can do the work and move the needle on diversity hiring, retention, and promotion/tenure rather than creating convenient and politically correct positions given the associated optics.

What Can We Learn?

While working in different parts of the country, Dr. Petitt has encountered similar legislation that works against greater inclusion and educational equity in higher education institutions. Given similar challenges in divergent environments, Dr. Petitt takes an institution's temperature, works at the pace the organization can handle, builds coalitions, and utilizes white allies to operationalize a diversity plan to effect needed organizational and culture change. Dr. Petitt succeeds by insisting on impact analyses of strategic decisions which consider how student groups may be impacted before a decision is finalized.

Notes

1 Gawunde, A. (2007). *Better: A Surgeon's Notes on Performance*. New York: Henry Holt & Co.

2 Audre Lorde was a Black lesbian writer, librarian, civil rights activist, and feminist who dedicated her life to fighting against the injustices of homophobia, classism, sexism, and racism.

Brandman, M. (2021, June). *Audre Lorde*. National Women's History Museum. https://www.womenshistory.org/education-resources/ biographies/audre-lorde#:~:text=Lorde%20was%20a%20professor%20 of,New%20York%20for%201991%2D1992.

The text quote comes from a speech Ms. Lorde delivered to a feminist conference in 1979.

Bowleg, L. (2021, June 3). "The master's tools will never dismantle the master's house": Ten critical lessons for black and other health equity researchers of color. *Health Education & Behavior, 48*(3). https://doi. org/10.1177/10901981211007402.

3 University of California San Diego. *The Chancellor's 21-Day anti-racism challenge*. https://diversity.ucsd.edu/initiatives/21-day-anti-racism-challenge/index.html.

4 Williams, D.A. (2013). *Strategic diversity leadership: Activating change in higher education*. Stylus.Williams, D.A., & Wade-Golden, K.C. (2013). *The chief diversity officer: Strategy, structure, and change*. Stylus.

5 The author's dissertation is among this growing body of scholarly work.

Mednick Takami, L. (2017). *Chief diversity officers in US higher education: Impacting the campus climate for diversity* (Publication No.10286152) [Doctoral dissertation, California State University Long Beach]. ProQuest LLC.

6 National Association of Diversity Officers in Higher Education (March, 2020). *Standards of Professional Practice for Chief Diversity Officers 2.0*. https://nadohe.memberclicks.net/assets/2020SPPI/__NADOHE%20 SPP2.0_200131_FinalFormatted.pdf.

7 Goldstein, D., Grewal, M. Imose, R., & Williams, M. (2022, November 18). *Unlocking the potential of chief diversity officers*. McKinsey & Co. https://www.mckinsey.com/capabilities/people-and-organizational-performance/our-insights/unlocking-the-potential-of-chief-diversity-officers.

9

"Education is the Great Equalizer"

Interview with Dr. Erika Endrijonas

Superintendent/President, Santa Barbara Community College District

A portion of this chapter originally appeared in *Women in Higher Education* in June 2022.

Dr. Erika A. Endrijonas was appointed Superintendent/President of the Santa Barbara Community College District on August 1, 2023. Previously, she served as Superintendent/President of the Pasadena Community College District from 2019 to 2023 and as president of Los Angeles Valley College from 2014–2019. We became acquainted through a CEO leadership panel on which Dr. Endrijonas served during my tenure at El Camino College.

Describe your job in one sentence:

Every decision I make begins and ends with whether it benefits students and contributes to their success.

What were the significant steps in your educational journey and career trajectory?

I started college planning to be a journalist. My first semester I signed up for a US History class and got an A on the first exam, but there was a note

Women in the Higher Education C-Suite: Diverse Executive Profiles, First Edition. Lisa Mednick Takami.
© 2024 John Wiley & Sons, Inc. Published 2024 by John Wiley & Sons, Inc.

from the professor. Being a diligent student, I went to the faculty member who said, "Please tell me you're a history major." I said, "No," and he said, "I'm going to make you one,". This professor became my mentor throughout college. He was the one who encouraged me to go to graduate school and pursue a master's degree and a PhD in history.

The first year of graduate school, I knew I was interested in 20th century US History and was in a seminar class when the professor, who became my advisor and chaired my dissertation committee, said, "Okay, everybody. Look around the room...10% of you are going to write for the other 90%". What he meant was that only 10% would become tenure-track faculty, and in that moment, I knew I was part of the other 90%.

I spent my time in graduate school trying to figure out what I wanted to do. The first year I had a teaching assistantship and the second year, I had a TA-ship that was related to becoming the undergraduate history advisor. I became the undergraduate history advisor, and on my first day, my boss provided training that proved interesting; he said we were going to walk around the university. We went into every nook and cranny, and he introduced me to everybody and helped me understand that the best way to be successful was to know everybody and know who to call when you have a question, etc. I was the undergraduate history advisor for a year.

After I took my qualifying exams and was conducting my dissertation research, I took an advising position in the College of Letters, Arts & Sciences where I advised 32 majors and specialized in pre-health advising; it was awesome, and I realized this was a significant way in which I could contribute.

At the time, my partner who was also in graduate school at USC, decided she wanted to practice law in Vermont again. We moved to her hometown in Vermont, and I got a job at what is now Granite State College. Granite State was one of four New Hampshire state institutions and was specifically focused on adults going back to college. I did what I call "cradle to grave" advising. I recruited students, did their financial aid, and advised them on associate and bachelor's degrees. I loved it! I finished my dissertation and was tired of being cold, so I got a job at Oglethorpe University in Atlanta where I was the Assistant Dean and Director of the University College, again for adults going back to college. I was developing a niche. I stayed about a year and a half, but my partner and I missed being in Los Angeles, so I was hired to run the L.A. campus of the Union Institute, also for adults returning to college. I was at the Union Institute for two years before landing my first California Community College job in 2000 at Santa Barbara City College. About two years later (in 2002), Peter McDougall, the then president, sent me to the Asilomar Women's Leadership Institute, which was an opportunity to hear from women college trustees and presidents.

Before that experience, I thought I would go from being a dean to becoming a vice president. I believed in the mission of the California Community Colleges, but I had never thought about becoming a president. However, I said to myself, "Wait a minute. I could do that job!" I recognized there were skills I lacked, such as fundraising and writing grants, so I dedicated myself to gaining those skills. I got involved in CCCAOE (California Community Colleges Association of Occupational Educators), a statewide organization; I was the dean on the curriculum committee for the 9 years I was at SBCC; and I taught throughout those years during each semester at CSU Dominguez Hills.

I did everything I could to prepare to be a vice president. In 2009, I was hired to be Executive Vice President at Oxnard College, which meant I was Vice President of Instruction, Vice President of Student Services, and the Accreditation Liaison Officer. I served in that role for five years and was fortunate to work for a president who really believed in professional development. I was not his first choice for the job (the Chancellor had selected me), but after two years he said, "Our job is to turn you into a president." For the next three years, I became the president of the statewide student services officers' association, I served on the CIO (Chief Instructional Officers) board, and I had written grants, so I cultivated the skills I would need to be successful as a president.

In 2014, I became president of Los Angeles Valley College and in 2019, I became president of Pasadena City College. I was president in a multi-college district where I reported to a chancellor, and now I am superin-tendent/president and report to a board of trustees.

My educational journey became realizing what I *was not*. I was not cut out to be a tenure-track faculty member, but I wanted a career within higher education. At the time, I did not know what my path would look like, but I figured it out. Through the course of my career, I have been an academic advisor, a faculty member, I have a PhD in history, and I was a career technical dean for nine years. I have a unique combination of experience. It is important to understand that you do not just go to a job for two seconds and go to the next level; you really invest in it, figure out what your weaknesses are, and affirmatively pursue getting those skills. This approach has greatly influenced my success.

Who had an important influence on your leadership approach and your commitment to educational equity?

I have always believed education is the great equalizer and levels the playing field. In graduate school, I remember having debates with my colleagues about the community colleges even though I had never attended one. The community colleges are the engine of opportunity for millions of low-income and first-generation students. Being in the community colleges allowed my inherent philosophy to blossom.

In terms of my leadership approach, I believe you learn as much from people who you think are doing a bad job as you do from people who are doing a good job. For example, I have an open-door policy, but the director I reported to at Granite State College would come into the office and was behind her door all day. In contrast, when I was working for Peter McDougall, on birthdays, he assured that a birthday card would arrive at your desk.

Every morning, I send an individual email to anyone who has a birthday. People are really touched by it. The EVP I reported to at Santa Barbara was a snap-decision maker and always changed his mind; he never took the time to consider everything. I never do this. At Oxnard College, the president was so focused on professional development. It is a small college, so he interviewed everyone from custodians on up. He always asked if they had their HS degree or GED certificate and asked them about getting an associate degree. He made it significant and important for everyone to reach for their highest potential. I have served as a mentor, informally and formally, for many people, including those who are seeking to change positions, a presidency, and our current employees.

I said to our managers recently that our job is to help our employees get to their next goal and to be their best selves, just like we do for our students. Part of this is that I believe in "paying it forward." This is so important, especially as women. I am here because so many women along the way helped me. Whenever someone asks me if I can help them, the answer is always yes.

When I came to Pasadena a year before the pandemic, I did several workshops for students and employees in our Career Development Center called MiLD, "Managing the 'I' in Leadership Development" covering different leadership themes. If participants filled out a rubric indicating a particular career path and submitted it, they could come and meet with me individually. I would review their path with them. I wanted to give people an opportunity to ask questions that they may not otherwise ask e.g. "How did you figure that out? How did you start that?" We also conduct leadership development workshops, and I hold monthly office hours for staff, faculty, administrators, and students to come to talk to me.

You are a major football fan. What role do you see athletics playing for students as they pursue higher education credentials?

I chaired the California Community College Athletic Association board, so this is my bailiwick! Student athletics is important because it represents the last chance for someone who really enjoyed athletics in high school to play on a team. That person may or may not have any aspiration to get to a Division1 school, but this is the opportunity to connect with a college community that is largely commuter. Community colleges generally do not yet have housing for people to connect in the same way as at a university. Athletics is a unique and important way that students can make connections and, at the same time, because we mostly follow NCAA rules, athletics is structured so that students will be successful and make progress toward their degrees.

When I got to L.A. Valley College and we were $5 million in debt to the district, most said, "Just get rid of athletics." I was not getting rid of athletics because we had just broken ground on a $36 million building, 300 athletes were already each registered in 12 units, and I was not walking away from that FTES (full-time equivalent students) or those students. In many institutions, athletics is one of the main ways the college serves our African American students. Athletics is important on many levels: students stay engaged, they progress academically, and they stay healthier. I bring in coaches who look at students holistically. Our football coach recently took a group of students for a retreat in Cambria where they did leadership development and all sorts of activities. That group of athletes will come together in a way that other students will not, given the coach's eye to the *whole* student.

We just expanded our food pantry and moved it into a larger space. The other thing I am planning by the fall is food kiosks. I want to create a mini food pantry in athletics and at our Rosemead and Foothill campuses. A student athlete survey was done a year and a half ago, and the number one finding was that student athletes do not have enough time to eat, sleep, study, etc. Why create a barrier in terms of their getting access to food if they may be food insecure? With our HERFF (the federal, *Higher Education Emergency Relief Fund*) dollars, our vice president of business services created food baskets that are placed in major offices and kept supplied with snacks. If students come in, it is not about asking them to prove that they have a need, but rather having the food available in case they are hungry. We are in a culture shift and offer a combination of basic needs services.

However, we still have folks who believe that basic needs is not their work. We must figure out where to offer those wraparound services around campus knowing that information in some places will be less than in other places. Over time, as more of the older faculty who do not have an equity lens begin to retire, we will see a change. California Assembly and Senate Assembly Bills AB705 and SB1456[1] changed the "you have the right to fail" mentality. That shift from access to success is where we are right now, and it is messy and hard because some folks still want to say that access is all that matters. The legislature and the governor have established that access alone is not good enough. The notion that "if you build it, they will come" does not suffice. If you build it, they will come but you are now going to greet students, find out what they need, and try to make them as successful as possible which is a very different mindset.

With the growing emphasis on data, we are shifting towards holding faculty accountable for the equity gaps and success rates in their classes. We did not continue a tenure-track faculty member a few years ago because, among other issues, the data showed that if you were a LatinX student in their class, you only had a 16% chance of passing; that is not acceptable. The real challenge now is saying to faculty, "Here's your equity data on this dashboard: Take a look. Ask yourself why one group of students passes your class, but another group of students does not?"

Our job as an institution is to disseminate the data, reinforce accountability by providing lots of professional development, and discussing what the data means. We have many DEI (diversity, equity, and inclusion) initiatives, but saying, "You have to be culturally competent" is not enough. What does this term mean and how are the competencies defined? How are we training people to be culturally competent? We encourage faculty to reflect on their assignments, how they grade, but a lot of people are still reluctant to ask themselves those questions and they need training to know how to ask those questions.

You have spoken about how you share parenting with your partner. How do you strive for work-life balance?

I am fortunate because my partner, Martha, and I have been together for 30 years. We met in graduate school. From the beginning, it was clear that I had far more interest in a career than she did. My career has determined where we live. It took us 13 years to have a kid. In terms of balancing, it is wonderful to have a wife, a female partner. We naturally do things e.g., she does the laundry and I like to cook.

When we had our daughter, I was working at Santa Barbara City College. Martha teaches at USC; she was teaching Tuesdays and Thursdays, so I was the primary parent on those days. It worked because our daughter could attend the child development center there. Once I got the job at Oxnard and our daughter was four, I drove Ava to Santa Barbara three days a week and then doubled back to work at Oxnard so that she could finish pre-school there. On Tuesdays and Thursdays, I paid two babysitters to pick her up. On Fridays, Martha would go. That worked out great until I became a president. I could control my mornings, but I could not control the afternoons, especially in the LACCD (Los Angeles Community College District) where I often had district meetings in downtown LA.

Martha changed her work schedule to Mondays, Wednesdays, and Fridays; I drive Ava to school, but Martha picks her up. At times, we have had to hire someone to get Ava to school if I am traveling, etc., but Martha was always going to be the primary caregiver; we knew that going into parenting. When I was pregnant and about to give birth, Martha asked if I wanted to stay home. I knew I wanted to continue my career. We had our family, but I never wanted to be the primary care giver. The reason our work-life balance works is that we are both very clear about the fact that I have the bigger job and more taxing schedule, and she planned to be the primary caregiver. It helps to be with a female. Our daughter is about to be 17 and attends a small, Catholic girls' school. We are the only gay family, so it is interesting.

You had been in your current role for just more than a year when the COVID-19 pandemic hit. How did the pandemic impact your leadership approach and operations at Pasadena City College?

There is no page in the leadership playbook for how to manage a pandemic! In late February of 2020, we saw what was on the horizon. It turned out our college had an "aerosol transmission plan" sitting on the shelf in case of a mass event. My special assistant to the president, who is also our PIO (public information officer), started meeting with people who included our college doctor, security, and others to begin discussions. Because Pasadena has its own public health department, we were in contact with them as they were also trying to figure out what was happening.

On March 12, 2020, we were supposed to have a spring professional development day where we were going to launch our Guided Pathways. We scrapped it. On the morning of March 12, we broadcasted on YouTube a message about the workshop we were going to do; this was the day before Governor Newsom issued the Stay-at-Home Order shutting everything down. I said to everyone that we did not know what the future was going to hold and that I knew everyone had a ton of questions. We began to focus on what online learning was going to look like because it was clear we were going to have to move in that direction. I emphasized that the information I had on that day was different from the information I had the day before and from the information I would have the next day.

What I emphasized to everyone was that we needed to be "Semper Gumby", always flexible. We did not know what would happen and we needed to remain flexible. The old adage, "perfection is the enemy of the good" applied. I emphasized we were all going to make mistakes in the weeks that were to follow, but that we were in it together. I was there to lead, "Semper Gumby", it was important to ask questions, new information would be passed along as it became available, and good luck to all of us! It was a moment where my job was to instill calm and to be honest i.e. "I have no earthly idea of what's going to happen but we're in this together." Between March 12 and March 18, 2020, we transitioned the entire campus to online learning and operations. The last in-person board meeting was March 18, 2020; in-person meetings did not resume until October of 2021.

What really helped at the pandemic's outset is that I had an awesome team! I had a great vice president/assistant superintendent, who oversaw business and fiscal services and administration, and who has since retired. His area was fully operational and emphasized what we could do and what we needed to do. We identified super users of our campus systems and distance education and paired them with faculty who needed help. I am really proud of what we did in terms of IT. Not only did we provide students with laptops and WiFi hot spots, but our IT folks also built a platform; if you were in a class and needed Word, you could access Word from the Cloud on our campus website. We set up a WiFi lot in one of our parking lots thereby increasing the WiFi so students could come to that parking lot to study.

Normally, the next installment of Pell Grants and other financial aid would be sent the second week of April. Instead, we sent all payments out the fourth week of March 2020 to get money into the hands of students. We had everything so well-established that when the first tranche of CARES (the federal *Coronavirus Aid, Relief, and Economic Security Act*) money arrived, we got that money out to students within a week. We did a really good job. I came to campus three or four days a week even though we sent everyone home except our custodians, grounds, maintenance, operations, and security folks. Several of my vice presidents were also here three or four days a week because I felt we had a responsibility to know what was going on in terms of our population, homeless people, and our facilities.

Semper Gumby. That became our theme. I sent emails to everyone encouraging them to embrace their inner Semper Gumby.

How has the pandemic impacted basic needs services for students and hiring trends at Pasadena City College?

We did a great job setting up a process for providing emergency aid to students, not just in terms of getting out CARES dollars, but we also have a generous foundation and there was already an established emergency fund. If a student reached out indicating a need for food, we figured out a way to get them a grocery card. I worked with our local lobbyist who reached out to our LA County Supervisor's office. Because many PCC students live in L.A. County but not within the Pasadena district boundaries, they had a hard time getting food from the local food banks. We worked with our lobbyist to ensure that *any* PCC student who showed up to a food bank could get food by showing their PCC ID.

We worked with Knox Presbyterian Church across the street because we did not have staff on campus to receive the 3,000 pounds of food we normally received from the food bank every week. We had food deliveries there. We arranged with Grocery Outlet so students could show up several days a week to get a bag of groceries. We expanded our telehealth program and we had mental health counseling. We really ramped up services. Last fall, we had 3500 applications for emergency aid, and we met every single one, from a need to pay a utility bill to getting a car fixed, etc.

In terms of hiring trends related to the 2020 racial reckoning, I had wanted to hire a chief diversity officer at the cabinet level prior to the pandemic. Our campus has done a lot of great equity work; however, the work was very much owned by student services. I believe equity is a campus responsibility, and the only way that would happen was by introducing a cabinet-level position where someone would take equity campus-wide. I got a lot of flak, and there were people on campus who were not happy and said they did not know why we needed this position. I said, "Well, first give me the grace that I did not just plop down from the sky. CDEIOs (chief diversity, equity, and inclusion officers) across the country do amazing work at institutions and we need that work." Our CDEIO started in Fall 2020, and her impact was felt immediately.

I also have a great HR Vice President, and we implemented what is called "redacted screening" for classified and management positions. When applications come in, all identifying information about the candidates is redacted; there are no names and no indication of where they went to college. We started screening employees without this information provided to reduce unintentional bias in the hiring process. We also changed our interview process for classified professionals and managers; rather than a single group of 18 asking all these questions, we did small-group competency-based interviews. A single candidate will spend now two to three hours (an hour with each of these small groups), and the small groups only ask questions related to the competency they are examining.

At the end of the interviews, the small groups submit their scores, and the purpose of the final meeting of the committee is not to compare and adjust scores; rather, the position finalists, based on a tally of the scores, are the finalists. I am very proud of our hiring. We are working with the faculty to try to get them to adopt this approach as well. We have 20 faculty positions open for fall 2022. We have hired six so far; one African American male, two LatinX women, two AAPI women, and one white woman. That is pretty good!

How did your campus respond to the 2020 uprising following the murders of George Floyd, Breonna Taylor, and Ahmaud Arbery, and what steps have been taken to address #AntiAsianHate and #MeToo movements?

The aftermath of George Floyd's murder was a leadership challenge on several fronts. First, I am a historian by training. I am not reactionary. I am all about context and studying things and taking in information before I make statements. There were folks who felt that I did not make a statement fast enough about #BlackLivesMatter. It was not that I needed to be convinced, but I was gathering my thoughts. I also attended a listening tour where raw emotion was expressed about how Black and African American students and faculty and staff felt they had been treated on campus. There was a lot to unpack, and it was very impactful for me.

Then we had a situation where the Academic Senate wrote a great resolution about #BlackLivesMatter. It was sent out in a campus-wide email. At that time, we had two adjunct faculty members, who were probably Trump voters, and they started an email war with the faculty and staff claiming liberal bias and racism. People really responded. After this went on for several hours, many people turned to me and said, "You should turn off their email." And I said, "I can't do that," and I took a lot of criticism for that. I said that I did *not* agree with them but cited academic freedom and indicated they had not said anything that rose to the level of violating offensive speech policies. Therefore, I could not shut down their email. However, I indicated that they could create an email rule to send these emails to a dedicated folder, which in turn, caused more upset. It was rough. Finally, I had the IT department create folders on everyone's computer to funnel the conversation. It led to changing who had access to all-campus emails and training on the difference between cc and bcc on emails.

Immediately, I had ordered our police department to no longer be allowed to use the choke hold and ordered a review of our general orders manual which campus police work by. We did reading circles; it was hard, important work, and pretty intense.

My partner and I have always felt we are "in it together". Martha was adjusting to teaching online. We are good at sitting, problem-solving, or just saying, "What's going on?" and having a cup of coffee in the morning together. There was a lot of processing which made a huge difference. We were in the parenting nightmare of the pandemic and trying to figure out the right way forward. There was always an understanding that we were in a unique situation that was not normal. There is still a small group of largely white faculty who are still mad that I brought back faculty to in-person teaching on January 24, 2022. I said, "Our students need you," but they are still upset and put forth a vote of no-confidence against the Board of Trustees and me in May 2022.[2] Some presidents wear a vote of no confidence like a badge of honor; I do not agree with that perspective. Instead, it has caused quite a bit soul-searching and resulted in me adding a monthly open forum and professional development to become a Trauma-Informed Institution with the Executive Team receiving the training first.

I issued statements on #AntiAsianHate, which also brought the ire of the two adjuncts I mentioned. Figuring out when and how to weigh into national issues as a community college president is challenging. We have a large Armenian population, so when Artsahk was attacked in Armenia, I made a statement. During the pandemic, an Armenian employee group came together, the PCC JAN (Joint Armenian Association), and they have done a lot of great work. The college has the Association of Black Employees (CABE), the Coalition of Asian Pacific Employees (CAPE), and the Association of Latino Employees (ALE). There has been a lot of attention on these issues. When crafting a statement on a national issue, I sometimes consult with our Board, sometimes with our Executive Cabinet, and always with our CDEIO, which is one of the many reasons I hired her i.e. to provide ideas on the types of things I may say in response. I try to get as many opinions as possible and have as many eyes as possible on what goes out.

What would you tell your younger self?

I would tell my 2002 self, "This job is as awesome as you thought it would be!" It is a hard job, but awesome and exactly what I had imagined.

How and why did you decide to pursue the Superintendent/President role at Santa Barbara Community College District?

Since I left SBCCD in 2009 to become Executive Vice President at Oxnard College, my goal was to return to SBCCD to serve as Superintendent/President. However, timing did not work well earlier because either

I lacked sufficient experience, or I had just started a new presidency. This year, timing worked well. I had wanted to accomplish additional things at PCC; however, a seismic change in the Board of Trustees occurring in June 2022 resulted in my no longer having the support of the full board. The board's desire to go in a different direction coincided with the application timeline and process for SBCC. While SBCC was definitely my first choice, I also applied to other institutions. Being selected to serve at SBCC has been an amazing "coming home" experience.

What advice do you have for readers interested in pursuing a path to a CEO role?

My advice is to get a mentor or mentors and be clear with yourself about why you want to be a CEO. In my career, the people I have seen crash and burn in these jobs did not believe in the work they were doing or the work that the college or system was doing. The people who have the hardest time getting to this level and staying at this level are those who want "president" in front of their name. They are the same people who will say in response to a directive, "Because I am the president." If you talk to anyone who has worked for me for the last eight years during my presidencies, they will tell you that I *never* say that. It is *not* about positional power. If you are not willing to explain why you are making a decision, if your answer to a problem is, "because I'm the President", then you are not making a good decision.

At the end of the day, it is not about the president. My job is to "President-proof" the college. If something were to happen to me, this college would not fall to pieces. In contrast, when I was hired at the Union Institute, the then-president, who had ruled for 17 with an iron fist, dropped dead of a heart attack which caused that institution to tail-spin for three years. I am replaceable. A student came to office hours the other day, and he asked, "How do you make sure you stay irreplaceable in your job?" I looked him in the eye and said, "You don't. You always keep in mind that you are replaceable." You want to surround yourself with people who are competent and do a lot of great things. You are there with them to be part of the magic.

What Can We Learn?

Dr. Endrijonas states that knowing what you *don't* want to do is just as important as discovering that which you do. She argues that negative leadership models are as important as positive ones in shaping leadership approach, strategy, and philosophy. On her career journey to a C-suite role, Dr. Endrijonas recognized key skill sets she lacked, and she committed to obtaining these skills including grant writing and fundraising. She became president of a statewide organization and benefitted from a college president who saw her potential and nurtured her professional growth. Dr. Endrijonas believes in the notion of paying forward her good fortune by mentoring others. She emphasizes that fostering our employees' future goals is as important as fostering our students to reach their educational and workplace goals. Dr. Endrijonas and her team's ability to navigate with maximum flexibility through the pandemic enabled them to maximize aid to students. She seeks to president-proof the college by keeping in mind that all CEOs are replaceable; the key is to build a fantastic team to share the journey and prepare for succession.

Notes

1 California Assembly Bill AB 705 requires that a community college district or a college maximize the probability that students will enter and complete transfer-level coursework in English and math within a one-year timeframe of matriculation. In lieu of assessment exams, one or more of the following must be used to assess students' for the placement of students into English and math courses: high school coursework, high school grades, and high school grade point average.

California Community Colleges Chancellor's Office (2017–2022). *What is AB 705?* https://assessment.cccco.edu/ab-705-implementation.

California Senate Bill SB1456, passed in 2012, enacted key recommendations of the Student Success Task Force to provide critical student support services on the front-end of their educational experience to increase student success by establishing policies to ensure all students receive orientation, create an education plan, and declare a program of study. The bill targets student success and support funds for the vital matriculation services critical to helping students progress towards their college goals, requires campuses to participate in a common assessment system, and post a student success campus scorecard as a condition for receiving student success categorical funding.

The Campaign for College Opportunity (2023). *SB 1456: The student success act of 2012.* https://collegecampaign.org/sb-1456.

2 Several participants in this book experienced a vote of no-confidence during their respective CEO tenures. Votes of no-confidence are brought forth by faculty members who usually believe the principles of shared governance and the role of faculty in decision-making have been violated. Available research suggests that while votes of no-confidence are symbolic, since an institution's governing board is the only body that can remove a president, the votes have a drag on morale and may bring a sense of malaise or paralysis to the campus community. See:

McKinniss, S. A. (2008). *Understanding No-Confidence Votes against Academic Presidents* [Master's thesis, Ohio State University]. OhioLINK Electronic Theses and Dissertations Center. http://rave. ohiolink.edu/etdc/view?acc_num=osu1211469170.

Evidence also suggests that votes of no-confidence occur during labor negotiations, times of change, or related to budget shortfalls and associated corrective budget measures. See:

Hill, R. W., Austin, W., & Young, B. (2014, April 24). *Vote of "No-Confidence" in community colleges: Badge of honor or kiss of death.* [Conference proceeding]. 98th American Association of Community Colleges Annual Convention, New Orleans. https:// nsuworks.nova.edu/fse_facpres/416.

Votes of no confidence are viewed as a major form of faculty resistance to presidential leadership. See:

Kezar, A. (2008). Understanding leadership strategies for addressing the politics of diversity. *The* Given the women CEOs' experiences in this book, a *Journal of Higher Education, 79*(4), 406–441, DOI: 10.1080/00 221546.2008.11772109).

This book suggests the need for further research on the question of whether votes of no-confidence have a disproportionately negative impact on women CEOs.

10

"The Pulse on What Matters"

Interview with Dr. Javaune Adams-Gaston

President, Norfolk State University

 **Dr. Javaune Adams-Gaston** became the 7th President of Norfolk State University in Virginia, an Historically Black College and University, in June 2019. In 2022, she was appointed to President Biden's Advisory on HBCUs. Dr. Adams-Gaston previously served as the first female African American Senior Vice President of Student Life at the Ohio State University. Dr. Adams-Gaston and I became acquainted through the writing of this book.

Describe your job in one sentence:

My job is to provide vision, strategic direction, and funding support for an institution geared to ensure those who deserve access, affordability and excellence can attend, be welcomed, and succeed in order to meet their educational and workplace goals.

Women in the Higher Education C-Suite: Diverse Executive Profiles, First Edition. Lisa Mednick Takami.

What were the significant educational and professional steps in your career trajectory? How did previous roles prepare you to serve as President of Norfolk State University?

I've been privileged in higher education to have served in multiple positions throughout universities and had extensive higher education exposure. I started out doing what I love—being a psychologist. My PhD is in psychology, I was licensed in psychology, and in fact, I had a private practice while also working in higher education for over 25 years. Before I graduated with my PhD, I was the director of the Black Cultural Center at Iowa State University.

When I graduated, I worked in the counseling center at Iowa State and then I went full-time to the University of Maryland, College Park as a counselor. As I became a licensed psychologist, I was 25 and about to turn 26 when I completed my PhD program. There were many things that happened along the way that propelled me in various directions in higher education, one of which was the death of Len Bias, a basketball player at the University of Maryland, College Park and the #2 draft pick in 1986. He had gone to Boston, returned to his residence hall, and died of a cocaine overdose. It was a big issue not only for the university, but also across the nation because it spoke to the question, "What do we know about how we are providing for the wellness of our student athletes?".

I had worked with student athletes at Iowa State, and much change occurred across the nation focusing on student development, mental health, and student wellness; we didn't use those terms at that time. I was invited to apply for a position in intercollegiate athletics, which led to me becoming the first Black female assistant athletic director at University of Maryland, College Park. My portfolio grew over the time I was there to include academic support, athletic medicine, strength and conditioning, athletic training, and all the career and developmental programs for student athletes. This was long before the current wellness model. We really thought about how to provide an opportunity for student athletes to be as successful as they can be.

We knew that athletes may tell their trainers some things that they may not tell their coaches; or they may tell the academic support person some things they would not tell their coaches about how they were feeling or experiencing issues and what help they needed. We thought it critical to help the enterprise of student athletes and coaches to understand the ways in which they could help student athletes feel they were successful and part of a team where intentional teambuilding was

centered. I planned to stay in this position for three years and stayed there for 9.5 years.

Then I went to the academic side of the house. A colleague called and encouraged me to apply for an open position as the assistant dean that, in turn, became the associate dean for our college of letters and sciences. It was the largest college with 4,500 students, all undecided majors, all the pre-professional programs, and we provided degrees. We had the opportunity to help students who came in undecided and had been languishing as undeclared for too long.

We built a series of learning communities. From the time the students matriculated, they self-identified with a learning community. They had classes grouped together and an individual studies class that let them think through and process what major they wanted to pursue while developing learning skills. One of the popular majors was business. Our business school was and remains well-established and considered, so many students thought they wanted to pursue business. Students' families told them they needed to go into business or engineering in order to be successful.

We wanted to form a relationship with the business school that helped students determine whether business is what they wanted. We had the opportunity for them to be part of the business school while affiliated with letters and sciences until they had completed a certain number of courses at a particular level to determine their direction. Students would say they wanted to be business majors but did not necessarily love the classes they were taking or perform as well as they would like. We had a great relationship with the dean and associate dean of the business school. We developed a joint program to help students identify and prepare so that if they were selected for the business school, they were already affiliated and had opportunities to engage, classes that were created, and an overall very successful opportunity.

Then another colleague called and indicated there was a job I had to pursue. The vice president for student affairs indicated that it was a job no one else would be able to get done. This role was related to career development. A wonderful career center had just been built, but they couldn't get the buy-in from the colleges to have a centralized career services hub for all students. Given my involvement with the deans' council, I knew people I could talk to and thought it would be interesting, given my psychology background, to see if we could move the needle on how to help students be their best selves in terms of being career ready. I knew that most students don't know what they want to do, and the data at the time reflected this uncertainty; the data indicated most students would change their major three to five times. We didn't want them to lose ground, but we wanted them to be exposed to what comes next. I had the opportunity to gain buy-in from all the colleges on how to support students. I indicated that students would not be able to clarify their paths and be hire-ready unless they had internships. They had to have internships because this is what the CEOs were telling us i.e. that students who had completed a successful internship would likely be hired, but if they lacked experience, hiring them would be hard. CEOs indicated they needed to know students would be ready to do the work related to their majors.

I pushed for internships and was asked to be in a meeting with the president's cabinet and indicated that every student needed to have an internship, and the president said, "Can you do that?" and I said, "Let me get back to you." What we came to create was called, The President's Promise, an opportunity for all students to have one of five experiences: a leadership experience, an internship, a research experience, an arts experience, or an education abroad experience. The promise of the president was that every student would have one of these experiences. Several years later when I was vice president at Ohio State, and we had lunch with the president (a different president) who said, "I know you,

you're the one who created one of our most successful programs, thank you!" It's always nice to know that people felt this was a valuable program.

From there, following a 20-year span at the University of Maryland, College Park, I received a phone call. Ohio State University was looking at a vice president of student affairs and asked if I would send my information. I'm from the Washington D.C. area, and University of Maryland, College Park was 10 minutes from where I lived. Both my older children were college level, but my youngest was finishing high school. I'm very, very close to my family. My entire support mechanism was in the D.C. area, so I finally said that I wouldn't be able to move forward, but about a week later, they came back and said, "Just send us your CV".

I'm really glad that they came back because it ended up being a wonderful opportunity! I went to Ohio State and became the first African American female vice president for student life. Ohio State has 66,000 students, 56,000 of whom are on campus given the medical school, the law school, and the veterinary school, the full array of graduate and professional students as well as undergraduate students. We had a very large organization of 40 units, 1200 full-time staff, 5,000 student staff. When I came to Ohio State, it was an opportunity to stretch and grow ourselves. We were able to create a new program called STEP, Second Year Transformational Experience Program. We knew we needed to have our students live on campus for two years.

We had a 2-year residency requirement, but we were never able to uphold it because we never had enough beds. This program required that we create 4,000 more beds, more dining halls, and a cadre of the university that would be effective in maintaining students to graduate. Research showed that if students lived on campus for two years, they were much more likely to graduate. I used some of the things I had used previously; the focus was to have faculty and students connected. The program that I cocreated in Maryland had faculty and administrators that ran the 1-unit course to help students clarify their paths. At Ohio State, we wanted faculty to run a 1-unit course that emphasized connectivity and enhanced personal, academic and career direction. The program focused on having faculty more engaged with the students outside of the classroom and how we could create spaces where faculty could come in and do seminars in residence halls on the first floor. It was an innovative idea, and it was costly, millions of dollars, but it was a university initiative. The provost and I worked very closely together along with the CFO.

The whole community came together to create this program which has been incredibly successful. We had financial support so that students could get up to $2,000 to do an experience (e.g. internship, research, study abroad); they had to write a formal proposal, the faculty would help them, and then the proposal would go to faculty review by the STEP program. If the proposal was approved, the student could receive up to $2,000 to engage in their experience. We knew these experiences would make a difference, but we could also help fund it to avoid the disparity between those with resources and those with limited resources for the STEP signature experience. The students were required to do a poster presentation at the end of the semester to describe their experience, which they named, "The Dr. J STEP Expo". It was really a progressive, experiential forward-learning program.

In 2019, Norfolk State called and I knew by that time that I would consider a presidency. I had relatives who had attended Norfolk State and had family from this area. Upon researching, I saw that this could be an interesting opportunity, and I didn't say "no" to them, and I'm glad I didn't. I went through the search process, and it's been a great opportunity because Norfolk is an HBCU. All the things I had done previously have led me to this point. I have a phenomenal executive team. My executive cabinet and cabinet are amazing. Several have come from other places. What they understand is that we can continue to raise the level of what this institution is and can be. I have been very excited about what my colleagues have seen and done in their careers that we can adapt or create here, or what other things we can design here that allow us to help students.

Getting the $40 million gift from Mackenzie Scott didn't hurt either! Our biggest challenges in HBCUs are funding and endowments. Endowments are a major issue; we were able to put almost all the Mackenzie Scott gift in the endowment.[1]

You have remarked that you consider your husband and three adult kids your greatest achievement. What impact did your family upbringing have on your career trajectory? What advice do you have on balancing work and family for aspiring women CEOs?

My parents were very focused on education. My father's mother had gone to college, and my mother graduated from college. So many people in the family were focused on getting an education as a way of moving forward. I have two sisters, one older and one younger. I visited my sister at college and got so excited, and I did the same thing for my younger sister, and we all finished and have had remarkable careers. My mother always told the story that when we were babies and the nurse brought each of us to her, she would count fingers and toes and then she would whisper in our ears, "You're going to college, and you're going to get a scholarship." I had a lot of support for all the things I wanted to do. I was an early reader which came from aunts being teachers, books always being around, and family always having books. I loved reading. I was not afraid to try new and different things and had a family who supported these explorations.

When I look back, I tried to give my own children the same thing. My husband and I met each other when we were freshmen in college. I was supposed to be at Georgetown, he was supposed to be at McKneese State University in Louisiana, but we ended up at University of Dubuque. We both come from like-minded families; his father and mother were big on education and made sure they all went to Catholic schools, and all had an opportunity to go to college. Education was seen as a through-put and for its own sake and value. Understanding the world and being a part of it was important, so education in and outside of the classroom counted.

We went through undergraduate and graduate school together, and we wanted our children to have the exposure to the world that we had received. My parents were big on world travel and making sure we had lots of experiences, so we did the same thing with our children. I look at them and think that they are amazing, incredible people! And my husband and I are still together, like each other, and love each other. It isn't a fairy tale. This is what I try to tell people. To be in a relationship, you have to commit to the work, and it's work all the time. It's hard for people to think this because they think a long-term relationship should be roses. It's nothing like that. It's making a commitment to the person and the relationship. We've been able to impart this to our children i.e. that the importance of being worldly and successful means you love what you do, whatever you do. Our children are a joy. What we are most proud of is that they still like us, they like us a lot.

Prior to your presidency at Norfolk State, you served as the first African American Vice President of Student Life at the Ohio State University. What significant mentors or sponsors have supported and your career journey?

When I was at the University of Maryland, College Park, there was a Black woman who has been an incredible mentor and has helped throughout my entire professional journey. I was a very young professional when I started there. At Ohio State, I had the opportunity from the then president to be selected to serve as the vice president, and he continues to be a great supporter. When he left, the new president promoted me to Senior Vice President, and he was also an amazing supporter. One man was white and had been the president for many years in multiple institutions and held other roles for many years. The other was a black man who had served in high positions and as president at several institutions. They taught me the importance of being confident, of trying new things, of how to work effectively in teams, to be my authentic self and not hold back. I'm not a "hold back" kind of gal! Many of the teams I led were all men. When I was getting my PhD, I had a mentor who was chair of the department and head faculty person. This person helped me know that I could do things, be creative, be on board and on time with what I was trying to do as a psychologist. He was a phenomenal mentor.

You served in private practice as a psychologist for 25 years prior to your career in higher education. How does your work and training as a therapist impact your approach to leadership in higher education?

Being a practicing therapist allowed me to be a good listener and to listen beyond what a person is saying to get at their meaning and what they are trying to convey. In the presidency, you're always operating at the speed of light. You don't necessarily have the time to unpack things with people as much as you would like, so you need to listen intently and listen even more to what they may be reluctant to tell you.

You have remarked on the importance of strategic partnerships Norfolk State has formed with multiple stakeholder groups. Which key partnerships are you most proud of? How does Norfolk State partner with area community colleges to foster successful transfer students?

We have a relationship with Tidewater Community College which is a larger community college located just a few miles from our campus. That partnership is important to us. We're trying to allow people multiple ways to grow their academic and educational success. We have a partnership that allows students who graduate from Tidewater and other institutions to attend Norfolk State University. We want them to go through the process of graduating with an AA degree because we know completion is important for them. We are proud of our partnerships with these other institutions. We want those students to have the opportunity to transfer to our institution.

Also, there have been so many strategic partnerships that have been so helpful to us. We have a partnership with Dominion Energy that I appreciate. There are multiple things we agree to, one of which is to close the gap for graduating seniors from the university. One of our issues is that we lose students not from dropping out, but because they need to work to be successful. Through the Dominion partnership, students in their last semester can receive up to $10,000 as a final push to graduate. Initially, the funds are a loan, but if students graduate, they don't have to repay the funds. The program is highly incentivized to give students a final push to finish. We want them to graduate. Dominion also supports highly talented students for the summer bridge program and the other programs that they need along the way so we can move more STEM students through the system successfully. They've also provided scholarships. They've been great supporters.

We recently formed a relationship with Landmark. They gave us $5 million, $1 million for five years, for students from the local community to attend Norfolk on scholarship. We've been privileged for the support we've been receiving, but we've also been very strategic about knowing that our biggest issue will be closing students' financial gaps. We're always looking for ways to bridge these financial gaps.

We also have some funds that come from the state to bring students who are local, within 25 miles of campus. There's a program that allows these students to come to school and have their total tuition and fees waived so they can attend. These things help us to increase the freshman and returning classes, so our total number of students continues to rise in a time where many campuses are not seeing enrollment increases.

During your tenure, Norfolk State was named one of the Top 20 HBCUs by US News & World Report.[2] *The university has innovated in areas including cybersecurity and a master's degree in cyber psychology. What drives innovation at Norfolk State?*

Our people. Our staff, faculty, and administrators are so innovative. They have a real pulse on what matters and are interested in creating new opportunities for students to create positive change. Funding is among issues that has kept us back in the past. We have had many bright lights. We are a US Department of Defense Center of Excellence, which is attributable to our director of cybersecurity who is now our vice provost. She secured this opportunity. Our provost established our first endowed professorship. It's an investment in these talented individuals that make it possible for us to try something new and different, to set up a COVID testing lab, for example. The funds we received from Micron to name our clean room are fundamental in terms of the next things we can do. It's unusual to have a clean room. We are now setting up a lab not only to do Covid testing, but also testing for many other diseases, and we can engage more researchers. Those are the kinds of initiatives that drive innovation at Norfolk State University.

How did the murders of George Floyd, Breonna Taylor, and Ahmaud Arbery and the racial reckoning of 2020 impact you as a leader personally and as the president of an HBCU? How did Norfolk State respond?

It was devastating in a way that we had hoped we had moved beyond. To see that 9.29-minute video repeatedly was unbelievable. It is devastating that currently in the world we continue to experience this brutality. To see Breonna Taylor in her home, a great citizen, just shot to death for no reason. Those things made all of us begin to say, "We have to think there must be change". It impacted students in a way that many were unfamiliar with. They may not have experienced much of this type of behavior. Students, faculty, staff, and community were stressed, discomforted, concerned, and they wanted to do something powerful. During Covid, there were not many students on campus in the fall of 2020, but our student athletes decided they wanted to do a march for justice in the city.

They were able to organize the march. I participated, my husband participated, we had a board member who participated. They invited student athletes from around the Hampton Roads area including from the College of William & Mary, Hampton University, and others who attended and demonstrated their commitment. It was important to them that their voices were not left out of the concern that was prevalent for everyone. We had multiple town halls and opportunities when students came back to talk about and plan for what they wanted to do and see done differently. For me, this was a call to action. It was not enough to wring our hands and say, "This is so terrible." We had to do some things and talk to legislators and get people to understand how devastating this was.

In April 2022, you were appointed to President Biden's Advisory on HBCUs.[3] How has this appointment impacted you as a leader? How will this important board elevate the goals of HBCUs to provide the highest quality of education to its students and continue to be engines of opportunity?

The opportunity to serve as a presidential-level advisory board member means you have a responsibility and you must be laser focused on change. Our co-chairs are very focused on what we can accomplish in our two years. We're getting there. We have four areas of focus, one of which I'm co-leading which is "career trajectory" and how we engage the CEO world in ensuring that our students have the preparation and opportunity to be successful. It's been reaffirming because the advisory is largely presidents of HBCUs, presidents of corporations, and some high-profile entertainment people in the room all saying what matters is HBCUs, their continuity, and their ability to thrive.

What would you recommend to readers aspiring to become a higher education CEO or specifically the CEO of an historically Black college or university?

One of the things I tell young professionals all the time—since I've taught graduate courses where many people wanted to be the next senior vice president or the next president–is that there's a time and space for everything *when* you want to do things. You want to look carefully at your "why" and you want to look carefully at your "when". Being a vice president for student affairs is a 24/7 job; being a president of a university is a 24/7 job times two.

You need to look at your whole life and figure out, for yourself, what is the proper time and space you will have to give up or manage to do this job? This is a job that I love. My husband says we were appointed to serve this institution, and I believe it's true, but it doesn't mean it's easy. You can decide, "I can have young kids and do this job". I had young kids when I was an assistant athletic director and I was traveling all the time, but I had a great net. I had my family there, my husband was there, I had a great support net, so I didn't feel that I missed out on them. We talk about "The Village", but you *must have* a village. I always tell people that you want to make sure you have a village; if you don't have this village, you create one. If you don't have the family support you want, you create that support.

We all need a safety and support net. Knowing you have that net, choosing the time you want to do a particular job, or deciding to wait a little longer to ensure you can focus on the job and on other things important to you in your life, especially the people, requires discernment.

What Can We Learn?

Dr. Adams-Gaston stresses that aspiring leaders must have or create a support network and consider timing when contemplating leadership opportunities. She emphasizes that people and teams drive innovation through a spirit of experimentation and by creating new opportunities for students to effect positive change. Dr. Adams-Gaston links her training as a therapist to her ability to listen intently not only to a speaker's words, but also to the meaning they are trying to convey and an awareness for what they may be reluctant to share. Dr. Adams-Gaston states that HBCUs are most often challenged by needed funding for endowments and closing students' financial gaps. Dr. Adams-Gaston and her teams succeeded in attracting a Mackenzie Scott gift of $40 million and a Landmark gift of $5 million towards these critical strategic objectives.

Notes

1 Kent, J. (2021). NSU receives $40 million gift. *Norfolk State University News*. https://www.nsu.edu/News/Behold/Featured-Articles/2021/ NSU-Receives-$40-Million-Gift.

2 To be named as a Top 20 HBCU, colleges or universities also need to be part of the publication's 2022–2023 Best Colleges rankings. See:
   Historically black colleges and universities (2022). *US News & World Report*. https://www.usnews.com/best-colleges/rankings/hbcu.

3 The White House (Press release, 2022, March 31). *President Biden announces appointments to board of advisors on historically black colleges and universities.* https://www.whitehouse.gov/briefing-room/ statements-releases/2022/03/31/president-biden-announces- appointments-to-board-of-advisors-on-historically-black-colleges-and- universities.

11

"You Need to Look Up"

Interview with Dr. Joanne Li

Chancellor, University of Nebraska at Omaha

Dr. Joanne Li was named Chancellor of the University of Nebraska at Omaha (UNO) in July 2021. She is the first woman of color to serve as UNO Chancellor and the first Asian-American in the history of the University of Nebraska System to hold an executive leadership role. I became acquainted with Dr. Li through writing this book and an interest in elevating the experience of Asian Pacific Islander women serving in higher education CEO roles.

Describe your job in one sentence:

My job is to lead UNO's mission and to improve students' social mobility and workforce development.

Women in the Higher Education C-Suite: Diverse Executive Profiles, First Edition.
Lisa Mednick Takami.
© 2024 John Wiley & Sons, Inc. Published 2024 by John Wiley & Sons, Inc.

What were the significant educational and professional steps in your career trajectory? How did previous roles prepare you to serve as Chancellor of UNO?

In 2012, I became business dean at an institution similar in size to UNO. In that role, I had the opportunity to learn about many functional areas of the university and build important relationships. In 2016, my then-president said to me, "You need to look up." I said, "What do you mean? I'm working hard at my job." He explained that I was doing a great job, but I was looking *down*. He emphasized that sometimes leadership requires you to look up and out. He indicated that he was planning to nominate me to the American Association of State Colleges and Universities' (AASCU) and Association of Public & Land-Grant Universities' (APLU) Millennium Leadership Initiative. When I researched AASCU's program, I learned it had been established 20 years ago by a group of minority college and university presidents who shared the hope of bringing greater diversity to higher education executive leadership roles.

The turning point in my career occurred in 2016 because *I looked up*. I attended AASCU's program in Washington, D.C. Of course, we received a great deal of practical training, but the most significant learning took place through networking among the chancellors and presidents who attended, and the US Congresspeople, Senators, Harvard lawyers, and others who presented. At dinner each evening, a president or chancellor would present, and many would say, essentially, the same thing: "You don't want to be a college or university president—it's a horrible job. Really, it's not a job: it's a life." But during the second half of their presentations, they would often choke up and say, "Now I'm going to convince you why you *need* to be a college or university president." It was powerful and inspirational.

By 2016, these chancellors and presidents had been tested by history and events at their institutions, including the ongoing response to events like the shooting of Michael Brown in Ferguson, Missouri, in August 2014. Chaos, uncertainty, and unrest spread across the country around racism and issues of inequality, while at the same time institutions across the nation were facing multiple financial and public relations crises.

The summer of 2016 changed the way I looked at higher education and my career trajectory. I attended Harvard's Management & Leadership in Education (MLE) program in their Graduate School of Education for two weeks. The first week we studied theory which was crazy boring if I'm being totally honest, but it was worth it when, in the second week, we

were able to practice everything that we'd learned. The experiences at the MLE resonated with the advice I had received from my then-president when he said to remember to look up. I really began to understand it: there was somewhere else that I could serve on a larger scale. That turned out to be the best advice I have ever received—Remember to look up, to reflect, and to build connections.

After 2016, I became very intentional about professional development every year. I attended the American Council on Education's (ACE) Women's Leadership Forum in 2017, I attended the Wharton School Executive Education Program in 2018 with leaders from different industry sectors who had challenges that shared commonalities. The first course was called "Creating and Implementing Strategy for Competitive Advantage". In 2019, I returned to Wharton Executive Education and attended "Becoming a Leader of Leaders." This course emphasized that leaders are usually not born but made. The assumption rests on the premise that leadership requires intentional development. Recently, I returned to Harvard for its New Presidents Seminar.

All these experiences inspired me and helped guide my journey until 2021, when I embraced the opportunity to become the 16th Chancellor at the University of Nebraska at Omaha. I left my deanship in Miami at Florida International University and came to Nebraska and started a new page in my career. My journey and my reflections made me realize

I wanted to be in a higher education position where I could make an impact at the university-level and pay forward the kindnesses and opportunities I had been the recipient of once upon a time. My own journey has been influenced, changed, and saved repeatedly by so many, and this opportunity would help me honor all of those who had believed in me along the way. In short, I wanted *this* job.

What impact did your family upbringing and significant mentors have on your career trajectory?

Like all Chinese parents, my family upbringing stressed hard work. My mom always said to put my heart into whatever I do to come out on top. My dad always said, "A promise is a promise. Always honor your commitments." My dad passed away in 2014, but when I became a professor, he reminded me that the Chinese verb "to teach" is formed by joining the two characters of "to teach" and "to learn". The idea is that the best teachers are always also learners. My dad gave me the best career advice to remember that to teach other people requires you to learn at the same time. I'm always humbled by my teachers. In coming to UNO this last year, I have been humbled, but also inspired by our faculty, staff, students, and community members. Every day they're eager to share their expertise and talents and help make me smarter.

After 2016, in terms of mentors, I have had quite a few presidents, former presidents and chancellors who were so selfless in helping me. Every time I had a problem I needed to work through, they always made time for me. I would send pancake mix or other gifts at Christmas time to let them know I remembered them. I always asked what I could do in return. What they said was also very humbling. They always stated the best gift I could give in return was to become a successful president or chancellor: "Give back everything we've given you by making life better for others." I can't emphasize enough how touched I am by this country that educated me, provided me with opportunities, and above all, made me a better person.

Their support and advice helped me realize that a chancellorship is more than just a job: It's a calling. It takes all of us to have that positive attitude, make a difference, and make life better for our students. My beginnings are very humble. But the journey to becoming a university chancellor opened my eyes to the fact that the calling of higher education is a lot bigger than me—bigger than any one person, really. Important, lasting change should involve everyone. A community member asked to meet with me recently about changing higher education. He's well-achieved, probably independently wealthy, and said our discussion was his most important meeting of 2022! He prepared a PowerPoint presentation and told me he'd been waiting 20 years for someone like me to come and make changes. He wanted nothing in return but to meet, be heard, and work collaboratively. We align on many points to make higher education better for our students, and he volunteered to help me make changes. This country never ceases to impress me. There are so many people who want to do the right thing not for themselves but for all students and all learners.

How has your leadership style been shaped by being a first-generation college student from Hong Kong who struggled to afford college and went on to become the first Asian American woman to lead UNO?

I never quite thought of myself as the "first Asian American woman to...", but when I first came to UNO and attended a donor event, a young couple approached me. The woman began to choke up and was in a flood of tears. She was so touched by an Asian American woman coming into the University of Nebraska system as chancellor. I began to realize that my appointment had meaning. It gave hope, representation, and it spoke to many people. People see it as an historic event. Personally, I just see this position as one part of my professional journey, but I cannot deny the fact that by being the first, I'm in the position to give hope to a lot of people. It's so humbling. I never thought this little girl, who grew up in Hong Kong and never imagined college not to mention a PhD program, would have this journey.

In my office, there's a calligraphy poem that hangs on my wall. The most important line is the last one: "I always live my life as if I'm the poorest one in the room." Every day I count my blessings.

I come to this position with a lot of empathy and understanding for the challenges our students face daily. For example, when looking at why a student got, say, a C rather than a B, there is more than just the classroom details to consider. Maybe that student works 40 or even 50 hours a week or takes care of their younger siblings. Perhaps that student supports parents who have substance abuse issues, *and* still makes time to go to school. Within that context, that student receiving a C is outstanding!

I have been actively trying to change the culture in higher education. After you build a stable foundation that lets you consistently provide excellent academic support, your responsibility then should be expanding that foundation into a scalable operation so you can reach as many students as possible. Higher education has the power to transform lives and improve the economic and social mobility of learners. Because I have experienced many of the same challenges our students face, I am dedicated to creating a space where they can feel like they belong. Our job is not to pity our students, but to show them compassion, dedication, and serve their needs. Every student coming in, regardless of their circumstances, is a winner. Our job is to help those winners reach the finish line.

Your background is in finance. You have remarked on students getting a credit card, always paying off monthly credit card payments, tracking their credit scores, and taking full advantage of employer-provided investment opportunities. How does your finance background impact your work with all university stakeholders?

To fulfill our mission and vision in a sustainable fashion, we must be fiscally responsible, operate within the constraints of our financial resources, and exercise the accounting concept of "ongoing concern". As a finance professor and a CFA by training, I know that we do not want to expend all our resources to fix problems in the short-term because we have the ongoing concern of the institution to sustain. As Harvard's former president, Larry Bacow[1] has suggested, if an economist says you can operate with unlimited resources, fantastic, but in higher education most often we are constrained by financial resources.

The finance side of the house provides guidance and discipline, strategic discipline. Strategy is often about what not to do. For example, if I'm given $10, I must consider where I should put that $10 to have a ripple effect in ROI to bring back and influence other parts of our vision. The training and respect for financial discipline allows higher ed to make tough choices. Just like any household, if you don't have the money, you don't spend it. My background helps me understand the need to balance considerations: In what areas can we save? Where can we leverage resources that we have available, and where are those resources best invested? Our goal is to manage risk and ensure the institution's ongoing concern. I often ask my vice chancellors to look at their processes and contracting to see where we can save costs, create enterprise solutions, and increase revenue. For every single dollar we can save, we invest on the student success side of the house.

Data suggest 30% of UNO students are Pell-grant eligible, 36.8% are first-generation, and approximately 30.3% are racially diverse.[2] Given UNO is a predominantly-white institution (PWI), what steps is your leadership team taking to address outreach, access, and affordability to increase the number of undergraduate and graduate students of color?

Empirical research suggests we must attract diverse faculty and staff to inspire students to believe UNO is *their* house, that they belong and feel comfortable. As poet Maya Angelou has said, "In diversity, there is beauty, and there is strength." At UNO, we need to launch areas to attract traditionally under-represented scholars and staff, and we must compete with all the other universities. Philosophically, attracting a diverse, more representative group of scholars is not only about UNO per se, but also about the community overall. As Omaha's metropolitan university, we want to ensure we represent Omaha, after all.

UNO has been a strong partner to the state of Nebraska and Omaha, which is developing an "Urban Core". This means figuring out how we can provide our students and colleagues a pleasant living environment to work or study, fun facts, and community events to bring people in so they see they can attend rap concerts, opera, or Sunday flag or kick football for their kids. It means providing ways to be involved and active with the community. First, at UNO we want to create an environment where "all are welcome", and we have to play in concert with what's already in place. We have a great mayor, Jean Stothert, and community leaders who understand that candidates want to work where they live rather than live where they work. We need to tap into this new generation of scholars and learners who have a strong sense of community. Second, in terms of providing affordability and accessibility to attract diverse students, we're going to expand into border states to provide very affordable and much more competitive tuition for students.

Third, resolving the cost of higher education is not only about tuition but also affordable cost of living. Omaha is a very affordable city. Granted, we had a housing crisis in terms of short supply, but we're *not* San Diego. You can find affordable housing here. We must start programs that attract young students. For example, we lowered textbook costs and have increased access to online educational resources (OER) thanks to collaboration between our library, the campus bookstore, and digital learning teams. This has been a major initiative that has saved our students $2.9 million in textbook and material costs since 2019! Our vision is that materials will be cheaper and remain open access. Students will spend $40 rather than $600 or more per semester on books and related materials. And when students don't have to worry as much about costs, they are better able to focus on their studies and finish their programs. Also, there are other activities in the UNO community, and many would like to present programs to our students and their parents. Omaha has something to offer everyone. Our goal is to create a natural congregation for the student body.

Omaha has a very philanthropic culture. There are many private and family foundations, donors, and community members who want to do the right thing. There are many UNO initiatives working to ensure that UNO meets the needs of traditionally underserved students. Many students will come to UNO on a scholarship whether as ROTC scholars, Scotts Scholars, Thompson Learning Community "Buffett" Scholars, Project Achieve students, or Young Scholars. What I have found in my time here is that many Omaha donors are willing to fund the entire higher education experience so students can move forward in their journey. UNO is a magical place.

You have commented on the importance of partnering with community colleges to meet Nebraska's workforce needs. What strategic partnerships do you envision or are in progress toward providing higher education which balances STEM and critical thinking skills and seeks to meet the state's unfilled job vacancies?

Community colleges are natural partners for urban universities by construction. Most students coming to an urban university are looking for an affordable education whether they come as first-year or transfer students. Our community college partners offer a very good alternative for the first two years of a student's academic journey. We have a strong intake of transfer students from community colleges, but we're not quite there yet in terms of a strong, established transfer pipeline. Over the last year, we conducted a data analysis and believe we can do more to expand the community college-to-UNO transfer pipeline.

Dr. Richard Klein oversees the student performance and enrollment side of the house as Vice Chancellor for Institutional Effectiveness and Student Success. Based on data findings, we recently visited many potential community college partners, met with their presidents, and added advisors for two major partners, Metropolitan Community College, and Iowa Western Community College. And we are expanding our partnerships as we speak. We asked what the transfer market is seeking. Hastings College, a different partner which is private, requires third year students to study abroad. Some students cannot afford this requirement or don't want to study abroad. So, we are working on a partnership with them to develop a "Study Away" program where these students can attend UNO classes to meet that requirement, and we can also arrange internships for them.

Many community colleges recognize that coming to UNO would be good for their students. We want to think outside the box with our strategic partners. For example, we may share common donors. Can we approach the donors together as a pair? Is there some need to support a project within the state, for example, educating and training physical therapists, where a donor could come in and help operations at both campuses?

We must be smarter in terms of streamlining and articulating courses with our community college partners. We don't want to just accept an associate degree unless we're clear on what students need to complete their baccalaureate degrees. We must be much smarter about streamlining curriculum with our community college partners, providing effective, involved advising, and generating tighter articulation agreements between institutions. In this way, we can agree to accept 60 units and students won't have hurdles in completing their second 60 units to graduate. Our goal in these agreements is to make the academic journey as efficient as possible and optimize the university experience—because this will ultimately minimize the potential for students to drop out.

The STEM TRAIL Center produces more candidates and enriches their education experience with a focus on STEM. The STEM TRAIL Center engages with college students at all stages in their academic journey, younger students from the K-12 system, professionals with workforce experience looking to expand their STEM knowledge, and, really, people from all walks of life. We have a 1.9% unemployment rate in Nebraska. We need to bring in help and train candidates in STEM skills to help solve that problem. We also have a new division called the Innovative and Learning-Centric Institution. This division is going to allow UNO to enter the space of micro credentialing and stackable knowledge to reskill and upskill some of our current workforce. In the state of Nebraska, we're going to exponentially expand areas where Nebraska needs talent and provide opportunity to retain our workforce. If a Nebraskan is unemployed, or even if they are employed, they can come to UNO to reskill, upskill, gain knowledge, and open different career paths to avoid being in a dead-end job. A fulfilled workforce is a stronger workforce.

How did the murders of George Floyd, Breonna Taylor, and Ahmaud Arbery and the racial reckoning of 2020 impact you as a leader? How has UNO responded since then?

These events, starting with George Floyd in Minneapolis, saddened the nation. They also opened a window for me as a leader to have a better understanding of the grief and sorrow of my Black students. At that time, I was in Miami, and through my students, I was able to gain a deeper understanding of the full impact these events truly had. The killing of George Floyd on its own was a tragedy, yes, but along with the deaths of other young persons of color, the underlying issues of bias and equity were magnified to an entirely new level. I have always viewed the United States as a place of opportunity, and the impact of the summer of 2020 was a new vision and understanding that those opportunities are not always equally available.

What really strikes me about that time is just how raw emotions were. That hurt had grown so deep without being properly discussed that, as a country, we were caught in a time of not knowing how to move forward. And, of course, this wasn't just something that affected my students. The faculty and staff in my college wrestled with these complicated emotions. Like them, I was not immediately sure of the best way for us to proceed, but I knew that however we moved forward, it would need to be together.

At that time, I created an advisory board in concert with my faculty and our public health office. We called it the Racial and Economic Injustice Advisory Board. Our vision was to create a space in which all constituents of the college community, including our students studying remotely, could have a voice. This group allowed our professors to share personal experiences and over time we were able to talk and work through the raw emotions. We made sure everyone was supported. We found over time that the program helped make sure that students and professors felt heard, which is so important—the program helps everyone feel truly valued, because they are, even if, on the national scale they may not feel that way. That program was later published by the Association to Advance Collegiate Schools of Business (AACSB) as one of their best practices.

My time with that board really enriched my understanding of the challenges of many of my Black students. I grieved with them and felt the pain—but I felt more hurt for the nation because we entered a very dangerous time. A divisive time in which it seemed as though nobody was willing to listen and understand each other's perspectives. And these events only exacerbated that environment. But the days that followed also showed there was much to learn if you kept an open heart. It showed that to have any hope of lasting change or progress, we as a country needed to sit down and talk, to find a mutual understanding of lived experiences. As higher education institutions, one of our responsibilities and obligations is to really observe social and cultural changes and provide a welcoming environment for all our stakeholders: students, alumni, staff, faculty, and community partners.

When I applied to become chancellor, I was able to examine how the campus responded to the events of that summer. And I have to say, their messages of support and connection to each other were beautiful. That is one of the things I truly appreciate about UNO. It was great to see that, whether it was Florida or Nebraska—Miami or Omaha, there was a true focus on the wellbeing of our college and campus and communities. In fact, it was during a visit that I saw—and they are still there today—messages around campus saying directly "You are welcome here."

Since taking on this role, I continue to be inspired by our students, faculty, staff, alumni, and our wider metropolitan community every day as we continue to fulfill our urban metropolitan mission and ensure that everyone has an equitable part in serving that mission. I want every student and each of my colleagues to truly understand that Omaha and UNO is a place for everyone. I want them to know every day that they are seen, heard, and valued.

What would you recommend to readers interested in pursuing a CEO role in higher education?

To those interested in taking on a bigger role in higher education or a CEO role, I would recommend taking a moment to remember to look up. By looking up, you will begin to see a bigger picture. You will be able to connect the seemingly unrelated dots. These dots represent different parts and units of your operations. Study these points and study those people who are working in those units. They are your opportunities to bring agility and connectivity to the organization. Get curious about what your people are doing and ask many questions. Their answers open many doors for you to see what can be in place for the future. Work on your ability to persuade and your openness to be persuaded. A big vision requires many to come with you.

Once you have an idea of that bigger purpose, then actively pursue opportunities to develop a network of colleagues you trust and can speak privately and safely with. Consult with them and listen intently. They are your foundation of support because these colleagues can multiply the task of persuasion. Never shut down opposition but take on an attitude to displace others' belief by providing your viewpoint in the most succinct manner coupled with statistics and evidence.

Also, seek out mentors who will help you go in the right direction. Remember their advice comes from years of learned experiences. Reflect on these experiences and identify applicability to help you tackle similar situations. Professional development in higher education is very important. Invest in yourself and get yourself out of the comfort zone. Learn with people that come from different industry sectors who will help you grow as a versatile leader. A long time ago, perhaps having a PhD was enough. But today, running an institution of higher education requires candidates to observe culture, understand all functional areas, and create genuine connectivity. Do not forget to develop your successors and train people in your organization. Investing in your successors is one of the most important investments you will ever make in your career.

As a leader in higher education, as in any sector, our goal is to serve an institution of exceptional people. Your goal should always be to help your people achieve success. Making sure your people have what they need to succeed means having a deep understanding of operations and culture. To do this well, you need a strong network to bounce around ideas and people who can challenge you in a safe way, asking "Have you thought about this? Are you sure?" Surround yourself with people that share the same integrity and commitment. Promote a culture that encourages people to speak up and share ideas. Creativity and innovation can only come when you foster an organization that truly cares for its people.

What Can We Learn?

Dr. Li's career trajectory was propelled by a mentor encouraging her to look up and beyond her job as a dean. Many who work in higher education leadership roles can become stuck in the day-to-day grind of supporting our students and the institutions where we serve. By Dr. Li's adopting the lens of looking beyond the role she had to the role she aspired to obtain, she pursued multiple, high-level professional development programs. In the process, she cultivated a circle of trusted mentors and advisors to prepare her to serve as Chancellor of the University of Nebraska at Omaha and to lead with input and support.

Notes

1 On December 15, 2022, Harvard announced selection of its first Black president, Dr. Claudine Gay:

Moody, J. (2022, December 16). Harvard Hires Its First Black President. *Inside Higher Ed.*
https://www.insidehighered.com/news/2022/12/16/claudine-gay-become-first-black-president-harvard#:~:text=Harvard%20University%20announced%20its%2030th,assume%20the%20position%20next%20summer.

2 UNO Office of Institutional Effectiveness, "Fact Book, Academic Year 2021" (2022). *Fact Book.* 40.
https://digitalcommons.unomaha.edu/oiefactbooks/40.

Appendix

Suggested Further Reading:

Bensimon & Associates for College Futures Foundation. (2022). *Whiteness rules: Racial exclusion in becoming an American college president.* https://collegefutures.org/insights/whiteness-rules-racial-exclusion-in-becoming-an-american-college-president

Boman, L. G. and Deal, T. E. (2021). *Reframing organizations: Artistry, choice, and leadership* (7th ed.). Jossey-Bass, a Wiley Brand.

Brown, B. (2018). *Dare to lead: Brave work. Tough conversations. Whole hearts.* Random House.

Coven, M. B. (2022). *Writing on the job: Best practices for communicating in the digital age.* Princeton University Press.

Eddy, P. L., Sydow, D. L., Alfred, R. L., & Garza Mitchell, R. L. (2015). *Developing tomorrow's leaders: Context, challenges and capabilities.* Rowman & Littlefield.

Fasching-Varner, K. J., Albert, K. A. Allen, C. M., & Mitchell, R. W. (Eds.). (2014). *Racial battle fatigue in higher education: Exposing the myth of the post-racial America.* Rowman & Littlefield.

Gellman-Danley, B. (2023). *Leadership Lessons Learned.* Higher Learning Commission. https://download.hlcommission.org/BGDleadershiplessons.pdf

Gawunde, A. (2007). *Better: A surgeon's notes on performance.* Henry Holt & Co.

Women in the Higher Education C-Suite: Diverse Executive Profiles, First Edition.
Lisa Mednick Takami.
© 2024 John Wiley & Sons, Inc. Published 2024 by John Wiley & Sons, Inc.

Loehr, J., & Schwartz, T. (2003). *The Power of full engagement: Managing energy, not time, is the key to performance and personal renewal.* Simon & Schuster.

Nepo, M. (2004). *"Fighting the Instrument" in Suite for the living.* Bread for the Journey International.

Taylor, S. L. (1994). *In the spirit: The inspirational writings.* HarperPerennial.

Professional Development Programs:

Asilomar Leadership Skills Seminar: https://ccleague.org/event-calendar/2022-asilomar-leadership-skills-seminar

Association for California Community College Administrators: Aspiring CEO Program, Great Deans, Admin 101, Admin 201, Mentor Program: https://accca.org/events-and-programs/

American Council on Education Fellows Program: https://www.aspeninstitute.org/programs/executive-leadership-development/

The Aspen Institute: https://www.aspeninstitute.org/programs/executive-leadership-development/

Association of State Colleges and Universities: Millennium Leadership Institute, Executive Leadership Academy, Emerging Leaders Academy, Becoming a Provost, https://www.aascu.org/LD/MLI/

California Community College Aspiring CEO Program: Aspiring CEO Program | The League (ccleague.org)

Harvard Business School: https://www.exed.hbs.edu/womens-leadership-forum/

Harvard Graduate School of Education, Institute for Educational Management: https://www.gse.harvard.edu/ppe/harvard-institutes-higher-education-programs

H.E.R.S. (Higher Education Resource Services): https://www.hersnetwork.org/programs/hers-institute/

Wharton Executive Education: https://executiveeducation.wharton.upenn.edu/for-individuals/program-topics/leadership-and-management/

Wheelhouse Fellows Program: https://education.ucdavis.edu/wheelhouse-center-community-college-leadership-and-research

Index

Women in the Higher Education C-Suite: Diverse Executive Profiles, First Edition.
Lisa Mednick Takami.
© 2024 John Wiley & Sons, Inc. Published 2024 by John Wiley & Sons, Inc.

www.ingramcontent.com/pod-product-compliance
Lightning Source LLC
Chambersburg PA
CBHW050707060325
23030CB00017B/308